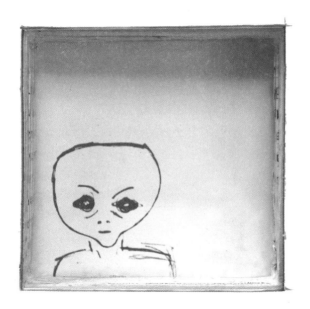

'If you've ever been on a night out where you got blackout drunk and have laughed the next day as your friends tell you all the stupid stuff you said, that's what being autistic feels like for me: one long blackout night of drinking, except there's no socially sanctioned excuse for your gaffes and no one is laughing.'

'Fern Brady's book is alive in your hands. Brave doesn't cover it and I'm not sure what will. Fizzing with intelligence, it will hit you in the heart, lungs and liver. You'll laugh, cry, be still and if you're not autistic – by god you'll learn. If you are autistic you'll be seen, heard, held, rocked and loved here. A set text for all of us in 2023'
–Deborah Frances-White

'Fern is a brilliant, beautiful writer with a unique voice and even more unique story. Astute, honest and very, very funny'
–Lou Sanders

'This book has the potential to truly change the way people think about people'
–Alex Horne

'So funny and brilliant'
–Holly Smale

Dedicated to Conor

Published in the United States by Harmony Books,
an imprint of Random House, a division of
Penguin Random House LLC, New York.

HarmonyBooks.com
RandomHouseBooks.com

HARMONY BOOKS is a registered trademark, and the
Circle colophon is a trademark of Penguin Random House LLC.

Originally published in the United Kingdom by Brazen, an
imprint of Octopus Publishing Group Ltd.

Library of Congress Control Number: 2023931387

ISBN 978-0-593-58250-3
Ebook ISBN 978-0-593-58251-0

Printed in the United States of America

Jacket design by Mel Four
Jacket photograph by Raphael Neal

10 9 8 7 6 5 4 3 2 1

First US Edition

STRONG FEMALE CHARACTER

FERN BRADY

HARMONY

NEW YORK

This memoir is my truth but to protect the privacy of others I have changed names and other identifying details throughout. If you think you recognize someone in here, trust me, you don't.

Contents

'What constitutes a problem is not the thing, or the environment where we find the thing, but the conjunction of the two; something unexpected in a usual place (our favourite aunt in our favourite poker parlour) or something usual in an unexpected place (our favourite poker in our favourite aunt).'

—*Jeanette Winterson*, Oranges Are Not the Only Fruit

Chapter One

A couple of times a week I'd have long phone chats with my dad as he commuted the two hours back home from his job in London. It was on one of these phone calls that I told him something I had dreaded bringing up since I'd found out a few days before.

'So I got diagnosed with autism on Tuesday.'

'Who told you that?' His tone implied disbelief.

'A doctor at the Lorna Wing Centre who specializes in diagnosing adult women with autism,' I said, already irritated that he thought someone had just mentioned it in passing or that I'd done an online quiz.

'Oh right. Traffic in London's mental, eh?'

(One time my granda had had his leg amputated and Dad mentioned it as breezily as you would if you were making small talk about the weather: 'Granda's in hospital and we think he's getting his leg cut off.' This was followed by a call the next day with a matter-of-fact 'Well, Granda's deid.')

I paced back and forth around the kitchen trying to keep my cool, my phone still pressed to my face.

'You know, I actually had a dream where I told you about the diagnosis and you were so uncharacteristically compassionate and nice about it that I woke myself up laughing.'

'Oh right. I had a dream that there weren't enough blankets on the bed, and I asked Julie to put more on 'cause I was freezing.'

I began to load the dishwasher while he continued telling me about his dream, oblivious to my lack of interest. I waited for him to finish before I said: 'Well, they say autism can be inherited from one parent, so I guess that's answered the question of which one.'

'Who? Your mother?' he asked in earnest.

I slammed a knife into the dishwasher in frustration.

'Are you kidding me? It's you! It's you, ya maniac! Have you ever noticed you've no ability to read social cues or people's emotions?'

Dad and I were similar in that we'd both run into trouble at work for pointedly telling people when they were in the wrong. We both had odd ways of communicating.

I tried to picture his response. I knew he was driving calmly, glancing blankly at the satnav, totally unbothered by any of it.

Mildly, he added, 'I dinnae even know what a fucking social cue is.'

'Right. Well, it'd be like if your daughter phones you up and says she's just been diagnosed with autism, a normal person would go, "Oh, and what's prompted you to get diagnosed? How do you feel? Are you okay?" You know? Any kind of response like that?'

I was shouting now. I liked talking to my dad because whereas I had to tiptoe around my mum's unpredictable moods, I could shout at him and his emotional response would still be flatlining.

'Well, I hope they went up and arrested your mother.'

I didn't know why I kept putting the same information into this computer and waiting for a different output. He wasn't capable of it.

'Why would they do that? Mum's feeling guilty about it, about how yous never got me help when I was younger.'

'She's the bloody autistic one!' Dad is now throwing the word around joyfully, like a child who's discovered a new swear word.

'I don't think so. She's had a pretty normal, human response about the whole thing and been dead helpful.'

'Right,' he said, sounding distracted. I could tell from the change in tone he was checking his texts.

Actually, Mum had been crying a lot since taking part in the assessment. She was full of guilt and had been going over and over how obvious my autistic traits were: like not wanting to be held or cuddled as a baby; or having special interests, such as teaching myself Danish when I was eight; or having violent meltdowns over the sensation of my own clothes on my skin. She felt bad the signs hadn't just been missed but were viewed as me being deliberately difficult. Growing up, I'd been told repeatedly that I was very, very clever but also very, very bad – and yet neither of my parents understood why I now enjoyed doing a job that involved people alternately cheering or booing at me.

'I'm still waiting for you to say one normal thing about this, Dad. There's still time.'

I could hear the cogs turning in his brain on the other end of the phone while watching the satnav.

There was a pause.

'. . . What did you have for dinner tonight?' he offered.

I leaned my forehead on a kitchen cupboard, opening and closing a drawer I'd smashed repeatedly over the years and had never been right since.

'Pad Thai.'

'Never heard of it.'

When I'd first got depressed, at 15, Dad had found me crying hysterically one night and had shouted to Mum in a panic, 'She'll be put in bloody Carstairs!' Carstairs was a high-security mental hospital in Scotland for serial killers, where they put away people who'd done stuff like skin people alive. Instead, I was given a half-arsed diagnosis of OCD and depression by my family GP after I'd asked him, 'I have obsessive routines and feel bad if I can't do them; is it OCD?' The GP's notes to the consultant psychiatrist in the referral read: 'Says she's always been strange.'

When I signed myself out of a teen psych unit shortly after my sixteenth birthday, I read the *DSM* manual[*] cover to cover and became an expert in psychiatry. I didn't think I had OCD as I didn't think I was going to die if I couldn't wash my hands

---

[*]   *DSM-IV* – the American Psychiatric Association's *Diagnostic and Statistical Manual of Mental Disorders* (1994).

15 times. Come to think of it, it was hard to remember to even wash myself anyway when I wanted to spend four hours doing French and Italian verb drills. The public perception of autistics is so heavily based on the stereotype of men who love trains or science that many women miss out on diagnosis and are thought of as studious instead.

In my binfire of a school, when teachers thought of problem kids they thought of disruptive behaviour. There was no such thing as someone who studied too much, even if they did give themselves a nervous breakdown in the process. It's only now that increasing numbers of health professionals understand to look for *intensity* of interest rather than unusual interests when assessing girls.[*]

Unlike many OCD sufferers, I didn't think not carrying out rituals would lead to my family being hurt – and anyway, I hated my family. They were so noisy I had to calm myself down in the evenings by punching my bedroom wall repeatedly or spending hours in my rocking chair. At no point did anyone question this textbook behaviour as anything other than me being annoying. One day I was doing my usual routine of spending lunch alone in the school library reading the *DSM* when I came across a thing called Asperger's. As I read the definition, I froze. It fit me perfectly.

The following week, with my psychiatrist, I brought up the possibility I was autistic.

'You can't have it,' he grinned, full of that jaunty misplaced

* Attwood, T (2015) 'Autism in females': www.youtube.com/watch?v=wfOHnt4PMFo&t=417s

confidence so many medical professionals have. 'You're making eye contact with me, aren't you? And you said you have a boyfriend. So, no, you don't fit the criteria.'

I now know that the diagnostic criteria for autism was almost entirely based on Hans Asperger's research into autistic males – and funnily enough, none of them had boyfriends because they were eight-year-old boys in pre-war Vienna. I didn't fit the criteria because I was making eye contact and anyway, I was a top student who'd just been accepted to Edinburgh University to study Arabic and Persian so what exactly was the problem?

At no point did anyone think to ask why I, with no prior interest in visiting or reading about the Middle East, had opted to study Arabic and Persian. No one thought it was weird when, after receiving my offer a year early, I self-transferred to a different school in sixth year to crash Higher Spanish and Advanced French 'for fun'. If anyone *had* asked why I chose that degree subject I'd have explained I'd simply run out of interesting languages to learn at school so on my UCAS forms I'd applied to study Sanskrit, Arabic and Japanese. I didn't want to visit any of these places; I just wanted to see if I could learn all the new verb drills. In fact, if anyone had asked, I'd have confessed I didn't really want to travel at all and had been banned from family holidays for several years by this point as I ruined them. I now understand that an aversion to holidays is extremely common in autistic people – the disruption to routine, the unpredictable nature of travel, the lights and noise of the airport and the extreme temperature change on arrival creates a special kind of sensory hell. Sameness is what I thrived on. I'm told that the appeal of holidays for most people is the novelty and break from the humdrum of everyday life. My family concluded among themselves that I was an arsehole. I didn't know why I was so unhappy on holidays either, so I had no other option but to agree with them.

After stopping and starting university twice, I began writing for the university newspaper, funding my unpaid work placements at various media outlets by moonlighting as a stripper. At the end of my undergrad I won a scholarship to train as a news reporter in England. Following an assignment where I was asked to try stand-up comedy and write an article about it, I quit the training and spent the next decade making a career out of stand-up.

Moving to England and starting comedy happened all at the same time. People saw me differently in comedy; I found they misinterpreted my shyness as coldness and my almost constant overwhelming anxiety as anger. I realized my loud, hoarse voice sounded stupid and was interpreted as aggressive by many English people, so I leaned into this new unrecognizable version of myself as an angry vulgar Scot. A lot of promoters on the male-dominated comedy circuit would try to touch the female acts up, so as a woman I figured it was better to make them scared of me with outdated national stereotypes than to try to be myself.

In 2017 I was filming a travelogue series around Europe and was at a gig in Berlin where I joked onstage about not fitting in with other women and having no idea why. A shy woman approached me afterwards. 'The stuff you're saying about not fitting in with other women . . .' she said. 'It sounds like a description of an autistic woman. Read a book called *Aspergirls*.[*] Please.'

I mentioned to my boyfriend that someone from my audience had said I might have Asperger's. I told him I didn't want to read the book. He immediately started to read up on the topic.

'This is you. This is like an exact description of you.'

'My friends don't think I have it.'

'Yeah but . . . you act like a different person around them. I've seen you in social situations where you're working incredibly hard to understand what's going on and follow the conversation. Plus, the way you are on trains and planes with the . . . the banging your hands on the windows and seats?'

'Oh yeah. That.'

I knew I had it. I knew it better than I knew anything about myself. But the psychiatrist had said that I couldn't possibly have it because I'd had boyfriends. Either he thought that all autistic people are unattractive sea monsters with no interest in forming meaningful relationships or he mistakenly assumed that the men I dated were capable of picking up on my autism rather than seeing it through a 'manic pixie dream girl' lens. A guy had called me a 'gorgeous weirdo' once and I knew instinctively that was good – that the 'gorgeous' part would help cancel out any potential discomfort with the 'weirdo' part, even if only for a little while. When I told all this to the doctor who finally diagnosed me almost 20 years later she rolled her eyes

---

[*]   Simone, R (2010) *Aspergirls: Empowering Females with Asperger Syndrome*. Jessica Kingsley Publishers.

in despair before I finished my sentence. 'You wouldn't believe how often we hear this from women,' she said.

On the Europe trip, a member of the film crew gave me Xanax to help me sleep on the flight home. I'd never tried it and was amazed at the total peace I felt. He gave me the contact details for his dealer and I bought a load of it. I figured I needed it as I had this weird habit of flipping out at home and destroying my furniture and wasn't sure why I did it. It frightened my boyfriend: a very quiet, peaceful Irish lad called Conor, who'd grown up in an environment of near-monastic silence by the sea. He'd noticed early on in the relationship that I didn't understand idiomatic language, which confused him as I seemed verbally articulate.

I knew I had it. I knew I had it but work was getting busy and my experiences as a teen meant I now loathed any involvement with medical professionals, so I ignored it and took more Xanax to calm down after gigs. I decided all I really wanted was to stop smashing stuff up. I didn't care about autism, which as far as I was aware was about how I communicated with other people. But the smashing of our stuff was exhausting. There are a surprisingly large number of doctors in stand-up comedy and I cornered a nice one at a gig after finding out he was training in psychiatry.

'Hey, do you know what the mental illness is where a person smashes things up for no reason?'

He looked alarmed. 'Er, maybe an anger problem? Maybe try CBT?'

I was already shaking my head impatiently. I'd done CBT all

through my teens and in the CAMHS* unit and no amount of calmly observing my thoughts from a distance could stop the feeling that my body was being taken over by a gorilla while I looked on helplessly.

'It's not anger, though,' I insisted, feeling panicky that a doctor didn't know. 'You must know what it is; you're a psychiatrist!' He just looked more uncomfortable.

So, I took more Xanax, sensibly balancing it out with the stimulant Ritalin that I'd bought illegally from a stranger on the internet called Sunset Sally. If a psychiatrist at a gig didn't know how to help me then there was no point going to the GP. I repeatedly googled 'Why do I smash up my house?' to no avail.

Trying to stop a meltdown feels similar to trying to hold your breath. Even if you can hold it for a while, eventually you have to resurface. I stopped buying nice furniture as it'd inevitably get smashed. My mum visited for two days once and immediately after she left I pulled a cupboard door off its hinges and bruised my hand from punching through it. No one was in the house. As I tidied up the mess in silence I thought, *That's weird. Maybe I found Mum staying stressful?*

One day I was having a meltdown and instead of shouting at me to stop, my boyfriend walked over and hugged me tightly. I calmed down faster than usual. 'Firm touch,' he mumbled into my shoulder. 'It's supposed to help.' Growing up, any time I had a meltdown my parents assumed it was a tantrum and would shout at me, but this only prolonged the whole mess. Unbeknown to me, Conor was learning techniques used to calm

---

* Child and Adolescent Mental Health Services, run by the NHS.

down autistic kids and testing them out on me. And they were working.

At a loss as to what to do and unwilling to have my partner work as an unpaid carer, I finally read the *Aspergirls* book. It may as well have been called *Hey, Fern, You're Autistic!* Imagine reading the most accurate horoscope ever, except instead of telling you that you'll find love this spring, it tells you exactly why you've felt like an alien for most of your life. It listed dozens of things I had thought were specific to my life experience and mine alone: misdiagnosis of OCD as a teenager; vulnerable to domestic abuse; low tolerance of alcohol; characterized as the bad child in the family; wrongly placed on antidepressants.

They mentioned a term I hadn't heard before: 'stimming'. This included hair-pulling, hand-flicking and – I shook my head in disbelief as I read it – spinning in circles. I flashed back to being kicked out of class aged 14. The teacher had come out into the corridor to find me spinning in circles and was inexplicably furious.

Just as quickly, I remembered being on the set of a panel show years ago. In between takes, while a makeup artist powdered my face, a producer listened to something in their earpiece before turning to me.

'Yup. Okay. Fern? Would it be okay if you stopped moving your hands so much?'

I looked at her, totally taken aback. 'Huh?'

'The director says you're just moving around in your chair a lot and sort of . . . fidgeting with your hands quite a bit?'

'Oh. I didn't realize.'

'Maybe sit on them?' She smiled helpfully.

I sat on my hands. I wasn't invited back.

Still, I continued to push down the thought of getting a diagnosis. There was no point in going to the GP. Encouraged by the rash of people in my industry and the media banging on about mental health and mindlessly mouthing slogans like 'It's okay not to be okay', I tentatively told a friend about how I had these times where I'd smash my house up, feeling my face go hot as I told her.

'And I don't really know why or how to stop,' I said, my voice trembling, hoping she'd say, 'Oh, I know just the therapist for that; they're great with women who inexplicably smash their houses up!'

She looked horrified and said nothing. I clammed shut. It was all pointless. Everyone else had nice, run-of-the-mill mental illnesses like anxiety or depression with simple, easy explanations, and for them it was positively revelatory that they could just take citalopram! Don't be ashamed to take your meds! And have talking therapy! And it's all okay. Isn't it so great we can all talk about this in such a liberal, open way?

Except I wasn't ashamed to take my meds and I'd been through the psychiatric system and I'd taken the pills faithfully for six years with zero impact. Prozac didn't stop me accidentally insulting people in everyday conversations; it just lent a zen-like calm to my delivery. I still didn't have any idea what was going on in most social situations, but the medication made me more agreeable to other people. I didn't think it was a taboo or hard to talk about mental health, but it was clear that whatever was wrong with me wasn't remotely part of the mainstream conversation.

It was also becoming obvious that I behaved in a way that was deemed socially unacceptable at work. I'd made the editor of a hipster magazine nearly cry on a phone call and wasn't sure why. I'd had meetings where the producers seemed to think I didn't like them because I'd asked what the point of the meeting was. People *really* didn't like it when I did this and would often say, 'It's just a general chat,' which was intimidatingly vague with no discernible outcome. If you didn't work out the purpose of a meeting it could mean you ended up meeting the person repeatedly – like the time I met up with a producer for years, wondering whether it was work or if she was just my friend now. There was also the time I let a pervy old agent phone me at nights and chat for hours without ever signing me as I didn't want to seem rude by asking him why we had to talk on the phone so often.

Gradually I came to understand that I was supposed to engage in a social game of pretending I wanted to meet the person not for work purposes, but for a coffee. I understood this was called 'building relationships' and it's where you pretend you want to be friends with someone in order to obtain the thing that you want. Sometimes you had to keep these games up for years at a time to get to work with them. It seemed nuts but I'd learned the world wasn't going to change to accommodate me so I started practising it.

Whenever I felt relaxed around people, I would let my guard down and forget to double-check everything I was saying as my curiosity and intense interest in fact-finding overrode the tiny, wizened corner of my brain that ran the social-etiquette programme. My friend Dom, a painfully shy Glaswegian actor who I'd known for years, mentioned the time I'd tried to compliment him on his weight loss by saying, 'Your weight really goes up and down a lot, eh? You're like the Kirstie Alley of comedy.' Another comic said that when I first met him I'd asked if he had the connective-tissue disorder Marfan syndrome as 'you have all the physical characteristics of it'. Hearing it recounted back to me a couple of years later I was mortified I'd hurt his feelings, but at the time I had just read the Wikipedia entry on Marfan syndrome and felt it would be useful to share it with him.

If you've ever been on a night out where you got blackout drunk and have laughed the next day as your friends tell you all the stupid stuff you said, that's what being autistic feels like for me: one long blackout night of drinking except there's no socially sanctioned excuse for your gaffes and no one is laughing.

Another time, a comedian turned up to a gig after the birth of his second child. It wouldn't stop crying and his face was droopy with exhaustion. I didn't know anything about babies or have any interest in them but wanted to make conversation and improve my social skills, so I scrambled for a fact that could be useful to him. I seized upon a *Guardian* piece I'd read on newborns.

'You know, sometimes a baby won't stop crying because when the mum is changing its nappy, a long hair falls off her head and gets trapped in the baby's willy. So, y'know . . . it could be that?'

The room went silent. The comedian made a sound like something was stuck in his throat. There was a blind person in the room too and I swear at that moment he regained his vision to stare me directly in the eye in a look that said, 'You stupid cunt.'

I gulped. 'It – it was in the *Guardian*'s Family segment,' I offered, grasping for some kind of credibility. No one said a thing.

Determined not to make these social faux pas again, I started studying social skills online. I watched a YouTube channel by a Swedish high-class hooker who made lofty proclamations about how you should behave in the world of rich people. In one video she insisted that 'a true lady never announces that she is going to the bathroom'. I nodded, vowing to remember this new rule that was going to change everything.

A week later I was filming a sketch. I knew by now that if I winced when people hugged me, or if I said I didn't want to hug them, they would see me as cold and avoid working with me in future. I was proud that I had already let the makeup artist *and* director hug me even though I found it unbearable. We were midway through filming when I needed a piss. I got up and abruptly left the room, confident in my new social expertise. After I left, the director said to the other comic, 'Is she okay? Why did she just storm off?' Someone had to explain that I'd just gone to the toilet.

At a dinner party with comics who had all gone to private schools and Cambridge I explained that I'd brought exactly 50g of cheese per person as that was the correct amount for a cheeseboard. I felt relieved that I'd got the social rules correct for once. My friend Luke started laughing at me.

'Who *knows* the correct amount of cheese for a cheeseboard?'

I was confused. This wasn't how this was supposed to go. I told him I'd checked in *Debrett's*, a manual for posh people by posh people. It felt unfair that on top of working hard at your actual job you had to also work hard to perform the right social rules but could still be penalized because they'd randomly changed according to some invisible whim.

I was so sure that, having obsessively loved languages at school, I just needed to do my social lessons like a French verb drill and I would pick it up in the end. If you could be fluent in a foreign language then surely you could become fluent in social skills. But it didn't seem logical – the rules of social skills weren't anything like as fixed as the rules of language. People lied and said things they didn't mean all the time or said one thing but made little bitchy faces to each other that meant another thing.

The first time I felt anyone else had the same feeling as me was when I heard a woman on a radio documentary who said being an autistic woman and masking (suppressing natural autistic responses) is like trying to speak a foreign language 24 hours a day.[*] For me, the pain comes in knowing that irrespective of the effort I put in, I'll never be fluent in the language of socializing. You can cover up a lot of the deficit by nodding and smiling but you'll never fully know what's going on at a party.

I quizzed Conor relentlessly on what people actually meant when they said things, learning that bafflingly when a TV producer says, 'We don't want Fern this time but maybe for the second series,' they absolutely do not mean 'for the second series' but are trying to politely let you down without hurting your feelings.

---

[*]   The programme was *Broad Spectrum* by Helen Keen on Radio 4 (2020): www.bbc.co.uk/programmes/m000mcyj

'So that means they . . . are being nice by lying to you?'

I was appalled this deception was considered a kindness. He sighed heavily.

'Well, no, Fern, because you call a lot of things "lying". You call some of my jokes "lies". Sometimes people say things because they find it uncomfortable to say what they mean. And . . . I guess they see it as kinder to not say what they think.'

By 2018 Conor and I had fallen into the habit of referring to me as 'somewhere on the spectrum'. The meltdowns were worse than ever but luckily I was on tour so I only spent two weeks of every month in our home – whenever things were tense it was time for me to pack my little suitcase and leave again anyway. For the hundredth time, I looked into and dismissed the idea of approaching my GP. I was too busy and anyway, I had plenty of money now so could replace the smashed plates and replaster the walls no problem. My arms and hands were getting bruised from all the meltdowns so I started weightlifting three or four times a week and developed a prodigious weed habit to calm me down. Friends said I didn't seem autistic. I smiled and nodded that they were probably right, then went home and smashed a chair into matchsticks.

I toured Australia and New Zealand for two months. I got one day off and instead of recharging, I decided to use that day to fly to Sydney and film a TV spot. After another two weeks in Melbourne, I travelled to Brisbane then finally back to Sydney again, where I played a gig to a couple of thousand people in the Opera House.

'The Opera House!' our producer said to me as we waited for our suitcases in the airport.

I wondered how much longer we'd have to be there and around people and lights and noise. I needed to just sit by myself for a bit.

'The Opera House!' she exclaimed again, sounding annoyed this time.

'Yep.' I had no idea what I was meant to say.

Everyone in our crew now was looking at me insisting, 'The Opera House! The Opera House!' – trying to force me to fake some sort of enthusiasm for this random building that would really be just another gig but with a fancy fruit platter backstage instead of crisps.

As an experiment I changed my tone of voice in the taxi to a bright sing-song.

'Hey, I just looked up this Opera House. It's pretty big! Wow, I can't believe we're gigging in the Opera House!'

They looked relieved that I'd finally given the correct response.

My voice had gone, my muscles were in constant pain from tensing them up all the time. I felt like a zombie. As I came offstage at the gig that night I told my agent I didn't feel right.

'But you did great out there!'

'But I feel weird.' The words sounded strained as I said them. I knew this was a big disastrous feeling so couldn't work out why it came out of me so tiny.

'Honestly, it was great.'

I tried to say I didn't mean the gig but shook my head silently, drowning out the sound of 20 excited performers and their agents chattering in the background as my vision closed in. Another four people tried to comfort me by telling me how good the gig was, as if any of this was to do with the fucking gig. I didn't know how to explain the thing that had happened.

A piece of elastic had snapped in my brain. The same feeling had happened at university and at school. I'd hear a 'PING!' like the timer on a microwave telling me: 'Time to go mad again!' Then the sound would fade out and I'd feel as though I was submerged underwater. I mumbled something about needing to leave and left the green room, running through a roomful of grand pianos tearfully, rattling locked doors and running down new corridors until I finally found an exit. I knew my brain had gone nuts again because in that moment I chose to phone my mum, something I'd normally find a test of my mental endurance. As soon as she answered I wailed down the phone like a baby. By now I was walking through the streets of Sydney, trying to find a street that didn't contain one of the two thousand folk I'd just told jokes to. I felt like I was never going to stop crying. Mum was crying too in her dressing gown back in Scotland.

'I don't know what to do when I'm this far away! I don't know how to help, Fern!'

'I'm just so *tiirrred*!' I wailed.

I didn't know how to say that this wasn't a tiredness I could sleep off. It was one that required me to sit at home alone quietly for maybe a month. Maybe six months. That was all I needed.

Before I went to sleep I posted a photo of me outside the venue on my Instagram: 'Played Sydney Opera House!' It got loads of likes.

I moved onto the final leg of the tour in New Zealand and got chatting to my friend's girlfriend, a newly qualified doctor who was specializing in psychiatry. 'I really think I might have Asperger's,' I told her.*

'Hmm. Well, if I were you, I wouldn't get diagnosed.'

'Really?'

'Yeah. Well, I mean, we're probably all on the spectrum to some extent.† Like, I probably fit the diagnostic criteria for it but with the government keeping records on people, do you really want that on record? Because they could use that sort of thing against you in the future.'

I nodded and tried to get on board with the idea of seeing it not as something debilitating that needed careful management but more of a personality quirk. Being autistic was just a kooky persona like one of those Myers-Briggs personality quizzes. Maybe loads of us *did* have autistic traits? I felt hopeful at the thought. So then did that mean everyone else was smashing up their house and crying in secret too? I could get on board with accidentally offending people forever as long as I could

---

*   I have ASD or autism spectrum disorder. If I'd been diagnosed a few years earlier it would have been called Asperger's but we don't call it that anymore 'cause it has links to Nazism and eugenics. I use it here 'cause it's what we still called it at the time.

†   It's a really, really common belief that 'we're all on the spectrum' and I think it comes from the misguided notion that the spectrum is linear. It's not like the Kinsey scale of sexuality where you can be a man married to a woman but you let a man give you a handjob once so you're a little bit gay. No one is a little bit autistic. You're autistic or you're not. The autism spectrum should be viewed as more of a big circle and where you are on the spectrum describes your support needs. Having said all this, I don't think it's too much to ask that NHS doctors know the basics.

gain control over the meltdowns. How was it that doctors could treat people who heard voices or thought they were Jesus, but no one could tell me, someone who was outwardly functioning well in most areas of my life, how to stop having meltdowns?

I loathed therapy. I usually only ever went for one session, where I'd do a decent impression of a normal woman, they'd offer me no solution and charge me 50 quid for the privilege. But I had an inkling the crying episode in Sydney wasn't ideal, so I searched for therapists who specialized in dealing with Asperger's online and found a charity that helped people who were pre- or post-diagnosis. I had maybe six sessions with this woman, who always wore an anguished look of concern I found annoying. Week by week, the same topics came up repeatedly on my part, namely: 'Can you teach me the right social skills?' and 'How do I stop meltdowns?'

I knew now from my reading that they called it a shutdown when you went silent or couldn't speak, which was what happened in Sydney. She kept telling me that I had to understand that social rules were changeable; I couldn't learn them all and I had to be more forgiving of my mistakes. She didn't give me an alternative. I refused to accept this. It all sounded well and good but in the real world no one was going to give me a second chance if I kept making these errors, so there was no option but to forge ahead. I concentrated harder on learning to be charming. Loads of people I worked with were total psychopaths yet their Machiavellian charm helped them get ahead in the industry, so I knew it was possible to fake it.

Meanwhile, the meltdowns continued to worsen at home. Autistic women are chameleons and can become brilliant at masking, but doing so is like having a computer that should only be running one or two programmes at once and forcing it to run up to ten. The computer will do it but eventually it'll overheat and shut down – and that was what was happening the second I got home and shut the front door behind me.

The therapist got me to install an app designed by the charity she worked for. It was called a grounding app and was intended to halt meltdowns in their tracks. I was delighted to have a solution. The next time one started I was punching the walls with one hand and opened my phone with the other. I went into the app, still panting, throat raw from shouting at no one in particular, tears streaming. Brightly coloured squares danced in front of me. I clicked on one hopefully.

Think of a dog.
Think of a delicious steak.
Think of being in the park with your friends.

I laughed in between giant choking sobs. I clicked into another part of the app, hoping there was maybe an adult section I had missed.

Take deep breaths.
Touch a soft cushion.
Think of a sunny day!

I flung my phone across the room, hoping it didn't smash again. I felt incredulous that I'd been naive enough to believe it'd work.

Another year passed where I tried and failed to be the best at masking. I realized if I left social situations early enough, I could control myself enough to appear normal-ish by going home before I got too burned-out. I stopped feeling guilty about not going on group nights out. I learned it was best to make media people I worked with think I was their friend and bring up things I admired about them rather than show little to zero reciprocity in a meeting. Instead of my preferred lunches alone I would arrange to have lunch with producers and act like we should be friends all the while feeling frighteningly fake.

The pandemic started and my boyfriend immediately had to work from home. I quickly realized the main reason we got on so well was because I only lived there half the time. When I was at home, I was out most nights gigging. Living with another person – not him specifically; any person at all – was intolerable. They move stuff! They're always there! You can't decompress, or stick to your morning routines, or be alone for as long as you need. He didn't seem to understand that living with me was as futile as trying to keep a pet monkey – they're cute and a novelty but inevitably they'll destroy the furniture.

Owning your own house in London is a dream come true for most millennials. Kicking clean through the glass door of your new house during a meltdown, less so. When a book on how to be in a relationship with an autistic plopped through our letterbox addressed to Conor, I finally filled out the forms for an assessment.

After seven hours plus lengthy interviews with my mum and Conor, the doctor asked if I wanted to take a break before she told me her diagnosis.

I thought for a moment about the correct answer. I felt my brain panic.

'Uh, do *you* want to take a break?'

'No, as long as you're okay to go ahead?'

I nodded. I didn't know the purpose of this back and forth, but I've since found out that a lot of this kind of questioning was also her way of assessing me. Normal people don't panic at the uncertainty of unscripted conversations.

'I'm pretty confident in diagnosing you with an autism spectrum disorder. If people ask, it's easiest to say Asperger's as that's more understandable to most people. Do you have any questions?'

'Do I have to put #actuallyautistic in my Twitter bio? There's a load of autistic people on Twitter and they complain non-stop and I just want to keep being myself.'

She laughed, confused. 'Some people are just annoying. It doesn't really have anything to do with autism. Don't worry, you're certainly unique.'

A few hours after the diagnosis I wandered into the living room. Conor was watching telly. I tugged at my sleeves silently, fidgeting, refusing to sit down. He paused the show he was watching.

'What is it?'

'I'm just – I think they made a mistake. At the autism place. I think – I dunno, they probably have to say I have it, don't they?'

He started laughing. 'No, Ferny. They don't have to say it. Remember they said they'd help you even if you had some other communication issue.'

'Well, how do we even know this woman was qualified? I'm gonna look her up.'

I googled her name. A string of articles came up. 'Dr Sue Smith, one of the UK's leading experts . . .'; 'Dr Sue Smith tells the *Daily Mail* about women diagnosed as autistic in later life . . .'

'What does it say?'

I slumped down in my chair.

'Uh . . . that she's a real doctor and one of the country's leading experts. Helps people in the criminal-justice system who've been misdiagnosed. Multiple letters after her name. Fucking . . .' I shook my head.

'Fern. You have autism. You knew this! It's okay.'

'Well, I don't want to have it.'

I knew now everyone would think I was stupid and every A I worked for in school and every effort I made to get my degree and every hard-won achievement would be invalidated by my diagnosis.

I wouldn't tell anyone. That'd be it.

Conor was already saying what I was thinking.

'You have to accept not everyone will like you and that some people love you for being the way you are.'

I stamped my foot on the ground. 'Conor no! I don't want to – I don't want to start being open about it. I don't want to be plucking my autistic beads and stimming openly. I don't want any of it!'

He was laughing. 'What do you mean? What are "autistic beads"?'

'They have special jewellery! That they . . . chew and things.

And you're supposed to be okay with it and start wearing wacky brightly coloured clothing or something.'*

I felt deeply grossed-out at the idea of being on the spectrum. Except – and immediately I tried to push this thought back down – any time I watched documentaries featuring autistics I understood that I was way closer to the people who 'looked' more autistic† than I was to the allistics‡ I was pretending to be like. There was a finality in understanding I was never, ever going to be able to navigate a social situation on instinct alone, or understand sarcasm, or suddenly be able to follow a conversation in a noisy bar.

A couple of days later I was lying awake unable to stop thinking about my dad's response to my diagnosis when I picked up my phone and tweeted:

> Got diagnosed with autism this week. Told my dad
> who responded by asking what I had for dinner so I
> guess this answers the question of which parent has it.

---

* This is likely uncomfortable for any unmasked autistics to read but society does a pretty great job at making sure we hate our autistic traits and I was deep in that state by the time I got diagnosed. Autistic people should absolutely have stim jewellery and wear whatever they want.

† I say 'looked' in inverted commas because, of course, there is no way to look autistic – but what I mean is people who either choose not to mask, don't have the capacity to mask, or have higher support needs than I do.

‡ Allistic means non-autistic.

It was late at night and I hesitated, thinking I'd delete it, but it immediately started gaining traction. I still felt totally ambivalent about telling anyone but had just announced it on Twitter. I worried about my neighbours seeing it and thinking I was mental. We'd moved to a recently gentrified bit of London and I really liked everyone there but only last week one of them had mentioned that the woman who ran our local organic vegan grocery was 'a bit on the spectrum' when she wasn't, she was just a horrible cunt.

I looked at my phone again and started to think of all the ways I could get cancelled. I thought maybe my tweet seemed flippant so I added:

> I'm not gonna go on about it and make it the only
> thing about me so I'll just share some resources
> I found helpful and not talk about it again.

The tweet went viral. Autistic Twitter was torn between being glad I'd been open about it and angry that I'd said I wouldn't make it my identity. I felt rising anxiety that once my industry knew about it I'd never work again.

'This implies she thinks she's better than us,' one activist tweeted. I was furious. I doubled down in my resolve to be the one person who could get diagnosed and keep everything the same. I would set the example for people who were autistic; I would never mention it or complain about it and I'd act normal at all times. Neurotypicals would *like* me.

This turned out to be almost impossible as the diagnosis had opened a floodgate. Everything I had avoided reading because it was too close to home, I binged on. I started listening to autistic podcasts every day; and when I wasn't listening to them, I was reading books on autism, watching autistic YouTubers, discovering autistic TikTok, chatting with autistic strangers online and joining Reddit forums for autistic women.

'It's okay,' one kind stranger reassured me in my DMs. 'Post-diagnosis you're gonna feel weird for about six months to two years.'

She was right. I had thought the diagnosis would make life easier. Instead, I cycled through feeling disgusted and embarrassed about it any time I told people, rather than relieved that I'd finally had official confirmation of why I experienced life the way I did. Occasionally, though, it was like having a whole new filter on the world. I struggled to see any positives from the label but by looking at autistic women I admired I began to realize that an autistic brain could provide an escape route from the traditional paths laid out for women. In turn, the problems experienced by autistic women sparked wider conversations around how society views women generally.

Autistic women speak out of turn a lot – that their direct honesty is jarring and unacceptable is a problem for all women, especially when we look at how #MeToo played out with so many women feeling unable to communicate consent clearly. Autistic women pursue their own interests obsessively – I come from a part of Scotland where women mostly exist as secondary characters in their husbands' lives. Autistic women have an almost childlike sense of injustice, meaning they are also often ahead of the curve in pushing feminist interests forward.

Honesty is powerful but it's not something that comes easily to allistic people because they're so driven to fit in with others that they prize collective values over truth. This is doubly so when it comes to women. Our autistic honesty is described as blunt or brutal or too much when really, at our best, we exist like the child in 'The Emperor's New Clothes',* pointing out what is false or hypocritical or a collective delusion.

Autism is partly a communication disorder and although we're not all 'a bit on the spectrum', many women do suffer from disordered communication.

---

* A fairy tale by Hans Christian Andersen, who unsurprisingly has been widely speculated to have been autistic himself.

Chapter Two

'By degrees I made a discovery of still greater moment. I found that these people possessed a method of communicating their experience and feelings to one another by articulate sounds. I perceived that the words they spoke sometimes produced pleasure or pain, smiles or sadness, in the minds and countenances of the hearers. This was indeed a godlike science, and I ardently desired to become acquainted with it.'

—Mary Shelley, *Frankenstein*

I come from a nothing town that you pass through on the train from Edinburgh to Glasgow. Glasgow has at least made a name for itself with its poor health outcomes and its lively characters – they really ran with the idea of the place being so shit it's good and they're all in on the joke. Bathgate has no such cachet. In fact, the only times Bathgate comes up in the public consciousness is in reference to its status as a place that's over.

It's in 'Letter from America' – the Proclaimers' song about economic deprivation in Scotland. When they sing 'Bathgate no more' they're on about the Leyland plant closing in 1986, the year I was born.

It's in a Frankie Boyle joke too, where he says, 'I was going through a town called Bathgate at night and there was a man pissing against the front door of a house . . . who then took out his keys and went inside.' When I went to university some posh guy would repeat that line to me over and over.

The biggest thing that happens in Bathgate every year is a thing called Gala Day. We dress as kings and queens and have a procession through the town before getting drunk and eating burned barbecued foods in our little identikit back gardens. They came up with the idea for Gala Days in all the old mining towns to give the workers something to look forward to so they wouldn't kick off. If you couldn't be a rich person, you could at least dress up as one. The mines were long gone, along with the Leyland Plant, but we still got to dress up once a year.

Even in fancy dress, I didn't fit in. In my eyes, everyone who fitted in and stayed in their home town was the real success. Imagine having the same friends from when you were born? Knowing and liking most people in the local nightclub? The feeling of community?

'I don't know what you mean!' I'd cry to my parents. (This is something I said a lot.) They'd laugh: 'I don't know what you mean! I don't know what you mean!' repeating it back mockingly. It didn't occur to anyone that I was very literally telling them I didn't know what they meant. My memories of feeling extreme anxiety go back to this time. Me telling everyone very clearly

I didn't know what they were saying or what they meant and them laughing as if I was a dickhead. It felt like everyone was speaking a foreign language and the frustration meant I had meltdowns, which further solidified the opinion I *was* a dickhead.

From the age of three or four I experienced a feeling I didn't have words for. The feeling was unease, a sense of wrongness, of impending doom. I babyishly named it 'The Bad Feeling of Life'. I imagined everyone had it and it was a part of life – just that no one had thought to mention it to me yet. In reality, it was constant anxiety compounded by the fact that no one seemed to know what I was talking about, no matter how hard I tried to communicate it to them. For most autistics existing in a world not built for them, anxiety is the baseline and constant background hum that their daily life has to play over.

My parents would tell me they were off to the pictures (a Scottish colloquialism for cinema) and I'd imagine them standing looking at photographs in an empty gallery. Out meeting my parents' friends, I'd be told to clap their dog and would tentatively place both hands either side of the dog and make clapping motions on its body. My parents would drop me off at nursery and I'd have to spend what felt like an interminable, purgatorial amount of time in silence as I couldn't think how to approach other children. Helplessly, I'd watch them play. I could no more speak to them than I could start speaking Japanese. Sometimes I stood near them in the hope words would come out or they'd strike up a conversation. I couldn't even begin to ask how to go for a piss so I pissed myself fairly often – and each time it happened my face burned with the same embarrassment a businessman might feel if he pissed himself at an important presentation. I was fine in my own home or even out and about with my parents, where I knew what was what, but at nursery the ability to put my most basic needs into words failed me.

We were all sitting on Erin's huge four-poster bed when she burst out laughing. 'I just realized! Fern has a moustache!'

The last bit of the word came out 'mousta-ha-ha-haaaash' as she bent over clutching her stomach in hysterics. Charlotte glanced at me and laughed uncomfortably. I stared down at my legs, horrified I'd been revealed as an aberration. I didn't really understand why it was funny.

Erin lived in a big Victorian house with her massive Irish Catholic family. Her dad was minted but sent the kids to state school and all the money leftover was spent on buying her the entire Dolce & Gabbana children's line.

Erin was in what they called the remedial class at school. She had large buck teeth that made it difficult for her to close her mouth. When I drew her portrait in art class I had to keep asking her to at least try and close her mouth over the teeth, like, *try a bit*, as I couldn't draw the protruding teeth without spoiling the whole picture.

The first time she bullied me I didn't understand what she was saying because of her speech impediment and my processing delay. She kept shouting, 'You're fat! You're fat!' at me in the playground while her mum, a kind woman called Margaret who was pregnant for about 15 years, explained hurriedly to my mum, 'She means "tall" when she says that; honestly, she means "tall" not "fat" – she just gets them mixed up!' Still, Erin talked to me more than anyone else so by default I figured we were best friends. There didn't seem to be an option in who was your best friend; they just picked you.

There was absolutely nothing I liked about her. She was spoiled beyond belief and we had no common interests whatsoever. My main interest was reading and she could barely read. She was remorselessly cruel to other underdogs in a way that made me flinch as I felt more of an alliance with them than with her. This is common with autistic girls: we often become friends with the most popular girl then mirror them for safety, clinging to them like a life raft for the rest of school.

I spent many miserable weekends at Erin's house. She'd walk us into her larder (her family had a larder!) to inspect the endless delicious food they bought in bulk before sitting me down at her kitchen table to eat packet after packet of Astros sweets in front of me, regarding me coldly as I sat empty-handed, unsure what I was supposed to do or say. As I hunched over in my chair listening passively while she insulted me, I'd try to work out why it was that I could read better than her but didn't have the capacity to stand up to someone who could barely pronounce words. It felt like there was a cleverness in my head but a slowness when it came to replying to insults. When someone insulted me, the Politeness and Nice Normal Girl programmes that I had to run every day in order to rub along with everyone overrode the other bit in the back of my brain that quietly said, *That's not okay*.

Before Erin, I was best friends with a tree in the playground. I felt a huge connection with the tree and walked in circles round it, talking to it quietly, stepping on its roots and patting it. This easily took up the full lunch break. I'd step on each root like stepping stones, circling the tree over and over while holding on to the trunk. Glancing up at the kids in the playground occasionally, it didn't seem like they were particularly relevant. Saying goodbye to the tree when I moved from the infant playground to the big primary school was emotional. I'd spent all week readying myself for it and trying to prep Tree as well. I knew it was sad too. 'Goodbye, friend,' I whispered, patting it.

Fifteen years later, on a quiet Monday night in the strip club I was working at, we watched a Channel 5 documentary called *Married to the Eiffel Tower* about a group of people termed 'objectum sexuals' – in this case mainly women who felt a strong connection to inanimate objects, so much so that they felt themselves to be in love with them. The women featured were all autistic. This was only mentioned in passing in the documentary, as if it was barely relevant to the spectacle of the format. I laughed along as we watched a woman smooch the underside of a rollercoaster or another woman whisper to the Eiffel Tower while straddling it; but later I watched the documentary over and over again by myself – not because I fancied inanimate objects but because it didn't seem so stupid to me to feel a connection with them.*

---

* Like tons of autistic women, Erika Eiffel, the woman featured in the documentary, was misdiagnosed with a personality disorder – in her case following a sexual assault in the army. Her romantic attachment to her archery bow and later the Eiffel Tower were dismissed as trauma/ fetishistic rather than a natural – and I'd argue, harmless – feature of

One day while I was talking to Tree, another child approached me, wobbling over to us and stepping on Tree's roots as if it had no feelings. I studied the child's face, their bowl cut and the green bubble of snot inflating out of their nose. They asked to play with me. I patted Tree anxiously to reassure it: 'Don't worry, we'll get rid of them in a minute.' I couldn't understand anything the child was saying, but after asking them to repeat themselves several times I figured out their name was Abby and we'd have to be friends now. This was always how it worked. I'd be on my own and people would impose their friendship on me whether I liked it or not. I wrote letters to her that had an anxious, instructional quality to them:

> Abby, please let's write letters to each other every
> week and let's say how many boyfriends we have.
> How many boyfriends do you have? I have eight.

Post-diagnosis I see this as the start of someone desperately trying to plan interactions with friends, to script the conversations so I could control both sides of the interaction and avoid the terrible uncertainty of girlhood – the vague offhand comments, the bitchy indecipherable side glances, the impossible social calculations, the helplessness of not knowing. Scripting is crucial for autistics. When you have no social intuition, you can use scripts to interact more effectively.

---

her autism. Her objectophilia helped her become an archery champion because she felt her bow was an extension of her body. As soon as she was open about this fact, she lost all her media sponsors.

There's a scene in *The Matrix* where Neo is programmed with every fighting technique in the world before opening his eyes and saying, 'I know Kung Fu.' There's a similar thing with autistic girls and literature. I had no idea what people were saying. I struggled with socializing, so by reading as widely as possible, I was arming myself with knowledge about people, about how they spoke to each other, learning turns of phrase and metaphor that others – even Erin – recognized. For years certain turns of phrase were physically uncomfortable to read as I couldn't make sense of them. I read 'lowering your voice' in many books and wondered why people were dropping to a deep baritone.

'Och, Maw, how are ye?' I said one day. I'd run out of novels to read so had been reading old Scottish comic books I found in the loft. I was hoping to approximate the Scots vernacular the rest of my family spoke instead of the stiff formal way that I spoke, which seemed to immediately let people know something about me was off. Instead, I was speaking 1950s Dundonian. My parents hooted with laughter at the oddness. Every attempt to fit in resulted in me being more weird and more isolated from normal people.

My sensory problems were also a daily issue. Everyone loved to retell a story about the time I was asked to be a flower girl at a wedding. I'd sit under tables at parties shaking my head listening to it, wondering when I'd get to tell my version.

'And Fern was so cute so, you know; that's why they wanted her there. And she had a beautiful dress on but *then*, for no reason, in the church she just roared and screamed the place down! Hahaha yep, yeah. Exactly like the child from *The Omen*!'

Here my other relatives would chip in: 'They had to take her outside and skelp her over the arse!' A chain-smoking aunt would say bitterly: 'I had to sit on her throughout the ceremony to keep her quiet.' The collective belief I was fundamentally evil had been solidified when I deliberately tore my pretty dress to shreds at the wedding reception while screaming the place down.

My recollection of it is this: a group of people stopped me from playing and put me in an itchy lace dress that felt like fire ants crawling all over my skin. They then braided my hair so tightly my entire scalp felt like it was being clamped in a vice. I ran out to the garden and frantically scratched my head to try and get rid of the unbearable feeling, the lace dress felt like a hair shirt. Someone beat me and dragged me back inside, tightly re-braiding my hair. I remember little of the church service but I'd guess that the singing, the unpredictability, the tightness in my scalp and the pain of the dress led to a meltdown that then led to me being beaten again and sat on. At this point in the story, the baffled adults would say, 'We gave her a pack of Chewits to calm her down and she wouldn't even pose for pictures.' I'd venture a guess that no one who has just experienced a meltdown is up for doing a photo shoot, with or without Chewits. These days I can barely get out of bed after one.

Early on, my mum let me choose my own clothes due to my point-blank refusal to put many of them on and my subsequent meltdowns. 'I had no choice.' I'd turn up to my school discos in a fluorescent-pink men's shirt, a woollen waistcoat, an orange shell suit, or head-to-toe beige – beige jodhpurs, beige jumper and beige boots. This look had nothing to do with '90s fashion. The clothes were never a trend.

One time I went skateboarding down our steep hill wearing bright-blue clogs – Mum had slapped my arms earlier and so I'd stormed out to do an extreme sport wearing clogs like any normal child. The combination of our road being on a 45-degree incline and my poor coordination in the clunky wooden clogs meant I fell almost immediately, fracturing my wrist. At the GP's surgery, the doctor finished putting a bandage on before grabbing my upper arm for inspection. He pointed to the long red welts forming, the skin broken in places. 'What are these?' I'd scratched frantically at my skin after Mum slapped my arm, trying to cleanse my system of the feeling. Every time someone touched me unexpectedly it sent a vibration like a tuning fork through my nervous system, making me itch and squirm all over.

I shrugged at the GP. He looked to Mum questioningly. She scolded me as we made our way back outside and into the car. 'Clawing at yourself again! They'll be calling social services on me! Thinking I did that!' I looked out of the car window, unsure of what to say. I had to scratch my arms after people touched me, especially if it was lightly. I *had* to. It was as second nature as blinking. 'They'll be calling social services on me!' she said again as we drove off. I didn't know how to stop doing something that was as much a reflex as coughing so I resolved to do my scratching and fidgeting in private, like going to the toilet.

'Do you remember me stimming?' I asked my mum, post-diagnosis. 'Hand-flapping, rubbing my fingers together, rocking?'

She paused to think.

'You were always clawing at yourself.'

It came back to me immediately. *Clawing at yourself.* This was the first time I'd heard it said neutrally.

Mum insisted on washing and carefully blow-drying my hair at nights, something I decidedly did not enjoy. 'Sit still!' she'd order as I protested and squirmed at the unbearable feeling of my head being touched and scratched with the brush, her smashing me over the head with the hairdryer to force me into stillness. As soon as I got into bed, I'd scratch my head frantically, mussing up my hair, finding it hard to breathe. Mum would crack open the door to check I wasn't doing what I *was* doing and then there'd be the terrible banshee screeching: 'You've ruined it! You wretch!'

I'd then be dragged out of bed, and my head stuck under the tap to wet my hair and the whole process begun again – only with more knocks on the head this time. I could hear the metal springs inside the hairdryer clanging while she cursed to herself that I was unpleasant, that I'd always been bad.

It's weird being brought up to think you're evil. I believed them when they said it – we're programmed to believe everything our parents say – but I thought being evil would feel more powerful, less lonely. Evil people didn't seem frightened of anything, so why was it that I felt frightened all the time?

One time in school we were talking about our mums. 'My mum batters me over the head with a hairdryer,' I ventured, waiting for people to be appalled by the abuse, to hand me the number for Childline immediately. 'My mum does that too!' shrieked another girl and we laughed. I don't want to paint my mum as a monster. This was standard Scottish Catholic parenting: children were not the longed-for IVF children of the middle-aged middle class – pampered investments that you needed to see a return on – but something dealt to you in life that you just had to cope with, like a cancer or a chronic illness.

School reports consistently came back with 'Clever but always daydreaming'. The truth was that in the absence of enough work to do I was being polite. I could already read – reading was all I did at home – and I did not wish to sit and pretend to learn to read with the others at an agonizing snail's pace. They tried to fix it by putting me in a special class with another clever kid (whose equally clever brother went on to be diagnosed autistic by the time we started high school, in case anyone thinks no one was getting diagnosed back then). They asked me one day if I knew the difference between vowels and consonants. The clever little boy answered. I said nothing and shat myself in my chair. After I shat myself in genius class I was quietly put back into normal classes. In terms of things that buy you social status and respect, having a high reading age is vastly overestimated. Not shitting yourself in your own chair is what's really gonna earn you the admiration of your peers.

The only good year in primary school was when we had an incredible teacher, Mr Rafferty. Mr Rafferty was drunk for the entire school year but to children this just made for an incredibly fun class. He abandoned the curriculum completely to teach us what he deemed more practical life skills.

'Now – let's list ways to avoid electrocution in the home. Can anyone name one?'

'Dinnae have a bath with a toaster.'

'That's right, Gordon. No baths with toasters.'

'Eh, dinnae put knives in toasters?' piped up a kid with crusty eczema hands.

'Correct.'

Mr Rafferty told us stories about his three-legged dog and one day he beckoned us to sit on the floor before bringing out a shoebox.

'I was walking my three-legged dog in the woods today and I found . . .' Here he leaned in, his voice dropping to a whisper. '. . . A little badger.' Kids jostled round the box trying to touch it but Mr Rafferty pulled it back. 'Don't frighten him. He might come out.'

The badger peeked out of the box. I felt like I might cry. This was the greatest day of my life. Every day, instead of learning handwriting or long division, we sat on the carpet and waited for Mr Badger to be coaxed out of his box. I felt immensely lucky as the closest I'd been to nature before this was when a Border Collie broke into the playground and ran in circles while we shrieked with delight.

As the school year went on, Mr Rafferty left us alone for increasingly long periods of time. I'd stare at Mr Badger's box but we'd been warned not to touch him as he was, after all, a wild animal and only Mr Rafferty could handle him. Mr Rafferty was still out at the pub or sleeping off his hangover one afternoon so I asked the two boys sat next to me what we should do. I normally wouldn't talk to them but I couldn't contain my excitement over the badger for one more second. They stopped their cackling and in-jokes for a moment and looked at me dumbstruck.

'That's no a badger, ya fucking fanny, that's a puppet in a box!'

I shook my head slowly, the room spinning around me as I tried to process this. 'No, it's not.'

'Aye it is, ya fucking spazzy!'

I got up and opened Mr Badger's box shakily, trying to keep my hand well away from the inside so he couldn't snap it off. I stared into the box, initially unable to process what I was seeing. In it was a manky old glove puppet on a pile of dead leaves. I nearly passed out with shock. I want to say this is normal childlike naivety, but it never wore off and from this point at school people learned they could say basically anything and I'd believe it without question.

Shortly after the badger incident, I overheard the art teacher explaining to the sub-teacher that they'd found out about Mr Rafferty's drinking. He was replaced by a stern English woman called Mrs Elliot. I was so distressed at the change that I tuned out her lessons for the rest of the year and fell into a deep depression. When Mum and Dad came in for parents' night, Mrs Elliot told them I hadn't done any work and was failing in everything. My parents went nuts at me in the car. It felt catastrophic. The only thing I was good at was being clever and I couldn't even do that anymore. Tears steaming up my glasses, I went into my room and looked around for a moment before picking up my little silk dressing-gown cord. I made a crude slipknot over the slats on my big wooden bookshelf. I put the loop round my neck to see if I could successfully hang myself from my bookcase. But for that I needed to stay kneeling down and every time I tried my legs resisted and I sprang back up, grabbing onto my shit life. I gave up.

I was eight.

We all had to read *The Hobbit* together in class. I found this intolerable; the world of pixies and elves and wizards was profoundly stupid to me and clearly wasn't real. The artifice of it drove me nuts. I didn't just dislike the book; I wanted to cover my ears every time I heard it read out. The teacher smiled as he told us it was his favourite book in the world. *You read it, then,* I thought. The length of the book combined with low literacy levels in the class meant reading *The Hobbit* took up the entire school year. Taking action on this theft of my reading time, I started sneaking my own books in to hide behind the cover of *The Hobbit* and drown out the guff about Middle Earth and Gandalf. I got caught one day and a discussion was had with my parents. I was given special permission to keep reading what I liked in class.

At lunchtime I'd eat my sandwiches in the toilets. I didn't know why, it just felt calmer there. When I got caught doing that, I was hauled in for a chat about why it was a dirty and disgusting thing to do. I felt mortified and didn't know how to explain that yes, I knew that but it wasn't like there was anywhere else for me to get some peace. Later, when I was diagnosed, Sue explained: 'Of course you ate your lunch in the toilets. The fluorescent lights and noise of a school dinner hall combined with the socializing was overwhelming for you.'

The feeling that I wasn't well liked in the family was always there. Every story was about me being, at worst, evil and, at best, brainy but sour and difficult to love. The only people who seemed to love me unconditionally were my mum's parents. My dad's mum was an absolute horror show in that she used Catholicism as a stick to beat people with. I called her Toodaloo because she used to shout it and wave as we left her house so I figured she was just shouting her name at us and it stuck. I didn't stop calling her this and it's still awkward now I'm in my thirties and have to ask if Toodaloo is dead yet or if she's still in a coma. My kind grandparents were equally as Catholic but they executed it in a hushed *let's not upset Jesus* kind of way. Toodaloo approached piety like they say Pope Benedict XVI did, like God's Rottweiler, continually making big belligerent pronouncements on the state of the world. It was weird she was married to our granda as he was drunk to the point of incoherence. The only thing they had in common was that they were both fat. She spoke in a posh Scottish accent whereas he spoke in a common one. She'd mock common people even though she lived in Bathgate and ate Findus Crispy Pancakes. Gran always gave the impression of a Hollywood starlet who'd been dropped into our area and was being forced to method act by living in a council house with a drunk. Any time I didn't pronounce the *t* in 'butter' she'd lecture me on the importance of something called the glottal stop while Granda drooled on himself semi-conscious in the corner.

In the summers we'd go stay in Toodaloo's caravan in Donegal with my cousins. We'd eat burned mince and potatoes every night.

'Granny, Granny, will you make my mince and potatoes into a garden?' my cousin simpered one evening. *What the fuck is she talking about with a garden*, I thought, jealous of their secret love language that I apparently knew nothing about. *When did this become a thing?* Gran smiled and leaned over Eva, pressing the fork tines flat to make fields in the potatoes. I guessed the sludgy mince was cow dung. I took note of Eva's babyish use of 'Granny' versus my more formal use of 'Gran', though, and resolved to do better.

Toodaloo doted on Eva, who was much prettier than I was. While I had quite nice eyes, they were obscured by my enormous milk-bottle specs, and the hair that sprouted from my eyebrows all the way down to my eyelids really took away from their beauty. I still had a moustache as well. Eva's face was hairless in all the right places – a key factor in being good-looking, I realized – and she was olive-skinned with huge Disney-princess eyes. Gran tickled her back for ages while we sat at the caravan table listening to *Doris Day's Greatest Hits*. I glowered at them from beneath my big eyebrows and thought, *I'd love to have my back tickled*.

'Can you tickle my back, Gran . . . ny?' I ventured, trying the 'Granny' on like an ill-fitting blouse.

She grimaced, opening and flexing her hand, glancing at me icily. 'My hand is tired now.'

The only time Toodaloo ever paid me a compliment was when I was fresh out the bath one day and had a towel wrapped around my hair. I was about to put my thick glasses back on to return to my de facto state of ugliness when she touched my arm, gasping. 'My god!' she said. 'You look like Our Lady!' Gran loved Jesus and in Irish Catholicism the tendency is to love his mum even more – so I smiled broadly, knowing that in the secular world this was the equivalent of saying I looked like Angelina Jolie.

Toodaloo pinned tiny silver feet on my jumper one day that matched the tiny feet on her cardigan. I was excited as these represented the size of a baby's feet when its evil mother wants to kill it and by wearing these feet we were showing our support for the unborn children of this world. At church I liked to look at the posters of dead babies in bins; it made Mass more exciting, though it confused me that my parents deemed so many TV shows and books at home as unsuitable but dead bin babies were fine.

For someone who was a passionate defender of the unborn, Toodaloo seemed to hate children as soon as they were no longer foetuses. Still, I enjoyed being around her in a weird way. Not because she provided comfort or warmth of any sort but because her constant declarative statements on issues like morality, etiquette, life and death meant you knew where you stood with her. No one else ever said what they meant, leaving life feeling like a series of unexploded landmines. This is what led me to say things bluntly, as it was the quickest way to gauge how other people felt. If you made a social mistake with Toodaloo she'd correct you in a way that ensured you never forgot: Sinéad O'Connor was the Devil Incarnate; gay people ruined a lovely word; only very beautiful women should wear their hair off their face.

One day I suggested rather casually that I didn't think I'd like to have children – something I felt to be reasonable chit-chat given I was ten. She slapped me hard across the face. 'You were put on this earth to have children!'

My maternal grandmother was more like a normal granny in that she openly loved me and wasn't repulsed at the thought of showing me affection. She was way harder to read, though, and could only communicate her displeasure through a series of throat-clearings, tuts and clicks that social anthropologists would be interested in studying. If I went through her cupboards full of junk and old toys from the 1960s she'd laugh and cuddle me. 'Raking around!' she'd say before handing me a plate of biscuits.

One day she did some raking around of her own and took me aside after going through my schoolbag. She looked mortified.

'Hen,' she said, 'I found some things in your – in your bag.'

'What things?'

She looked at the floor in horror and cleared her throat again. 'They're no good for ye.'

I had no clue what she was talking about but she cleared her throat another three times, each one more agitated than the last. Gradually, through me going, 'What? *What*?' and her clicking and muttering and throat-clearing, we established she meant my tampons.

'They're no nice, hen.'

I realize as an adult that this – like everything in my upbringing – was a hangover from our insane Irish Catholic beliefs: in this case the belief that tampons compromise your virginity. Because anything that goes inside a vagina must be like a dick, which is dumb 'cause if someone had a tampon-sized dick I wouldn't let them anywhere near me.

I loved my mum's mum but shook my head at her and left her glaring at my tiny cotton lovers. The belief that periods were some shameful thing was everywhere but luckily my incessant novel-reading told me they were normal and the world was just weird about them. I started mine at eleven and, careful to protect my mum, avoided telling her for three months until some thick fanny pads were tactfully placed in my drawer after I perioded all over the bed. Mum had weird views on periods too. She came into the bathroom when I was having a bath one time, looking uncomfortable. It was the same agonized look Gran had on her face when she did the throat-clearing.

'Fern . . . you know how sometimes when we go swimming, my friend Jane can't go because she's got a sore leg?'

I took a beaker and splashed water over my hair. 'Yeah.'

Mum grimaced, looking like she'd rather be anywhere but there. 'Well . . . she hasn't really got a sore leg.'

She looked at me meaningfully, something people would go on to do to me fruitlessly for the rest of my life instead of getting to the point and saying what they mean. I wished people would just tell me. I looked at her blankly. I was used to vague, nonsensical discussions in this family so I could wait.

'Right.'

Mum looked pained as if I was wilfully not understanding her. 'Fern. Jane is having her *period*.'

She said 'period' the way you say 'amputation' or 'chemo'.

'Well why doesn't she just use tampons?' I said coolly. Mum left the bathroom after that and I splashed around, reflecting on what a dork Jane was using fanny pads like a big baby. The tampon adverts literally showed a woman swimming, for god's sake.

Chapter Three

Once I got to high school I rapidly realized that girls preferred to say they hated you indirectly and that my habit of dressing in the brightest, maddest clothes possible wasn't helping at all. I still had my two best friends from primary school but they weren't so much friends as people I sat with so I didn't have to sit on my own. Erin's learning difficulty made her increasingly hard to relate to and I was beginning to understand that my other mate was a pathological liar.

In assembly one morning she whispered to me: 'So my brother's in therapy now.'

'Why?'

She looked at me as if it was obvious. 'Well, you *have* to have therapy after you've been abducted by aliens . . .'

'Has he?'

She nodded solemnly. I turned back to face the front.

'I'm sorry to hear that, then . . .'

When I mentioned it to Mum that night, she looked worried before reminding me gently to remember not everything everyone said was the truth.

I had begun to develop tactics to block out my classmates. When I couldn't follow any of what was being said in class one day, I grabbed a strand of my hair and pulled it over my face, looping some in a moustache between my nose and mouth while attempting to balance it there by puckering my lips. Concentrating on this helped tune out the noise of the classroom. Trying to pick out the teacher's voice was like listening to a distorted radio; I could barely make out what he was saying over the sound of 30 pupils whispering and tapping things and the piercing fluorescent lights.

I held the strand of hair close to my eyes, totally absorbed in the task of finding and pulling off any split ends.

'Hold on, everyone – Fern's just checking her Pantene's worked.'

I looked up, startled. Mr Graham, a kind geography teacher with a strong Lancashire accent, was smiling at me. 'You still with us?'

I nodded silently.

I heard someone burst out laughing. I looked up and one of the popular girls, Louise, was doing an impression of me puckering my lips to her mate. When I looked over, they dissolved into giggles, slapping the desk in glee. Most teenagers are cripplingly self-conscious, but it hadn't even occurred to me that anyone might be looking at me, never mind mocking me.

At lunch while the bell rang and rattled through me,

I huddled under some stairs at the end of the long corridor and watched everyone's backs receding. Everyone did their hair the same way. I liked spotting patterns and could see that first the popular girls did stuff and then everyone fell into line. No one discussed it; they just made a silent agreement and somehow knew. For a while, the trend was for everyone to cut a hole in a sock and then roll it into a doughnut shape before sliding it onto their ponytails to make a big bun on the top of their head. They'd pile colourful satin scrunchies on, their wrists straining as they looped the scrunchies round. It looked stupid but from what I could tell, the more scrunchies piled on your doughnut of hair the higher your status was.

A few months later, in the spring, there was a school trip to the South of France on the horizon. We were going to canoe our way through the Ardèche region. I pictured the whole thing in detail, which I always did with holidays to lessen the terrifying uncertainty they brought on. I imagined sophisticated scenes where I would sip chilled white wine and finally immerse myself in French conversation. The trip would consist exclusively of other straight-A students and we'd soak up Gallic culture, free from the bullies and the dun-coloured Portakabins we usually spent our days in.

From the moment the bus set off from Scotland I realized a terrible mistake had been made and the school had inexplicably taken part in some sort of access scheme enabling the roughest kids to come on the trip. Today, as a good *Guardian*-reading leftie, I'm all for this kind of thing. At the time, as a bespectacled open-mouthed geek with absolutely no ability to defend myself, spending 12 hours on a coach with these people didn't bear thinking about.

After the bus ordeal was over, we took to camping for the night. There were a couple of brothers in the school who were renowned for allegedly setting fire to their own house with their parents still in it. Out of all the people who could potentially find and steal my rusty, bloodied period pants from the tent, I'd say they were the worst possible option.

'You've got skiddies on yer knickers – ugh, you've *shit* yerself!'

'I didn't . . .'

I was sharing a tent with three terrifying girls from the year above. They fell about laughing and groaning in disgust. 'Get her out! I dinnae want to share a tent with that pure freak, man!' one of them shouted gruffly.

'Well, if you didn't shit yerself what the fuck's *that*?' cried one of the brothers, thrusting the pants in my face again.

I couldn't work out how to tell them I'd just started my period earlier than anyone else in school so I was faced with a horrifying Sophie's Choice: say I've perioded myself (downside: uncharted territory) or let everyone think I'd shat myself (disgusting but accessibly so . . .)? I was fairly certain either option would spell absolute social death. I imagined myself rising above it, saying confidently with a little smile: 'It's not shit, *actually*; it's period blood.' Rolling my eyes at their youthful ignorance. Then everyone would hoist me up on their shoulders, cheering at how cool I was, and make me head girl. Hardly. Mum, Gran and the story of Jane's sore leg had all made it clear that the topic of periods belonged in the folder of things marked 'Unmentionable'.

Instead, I tried to look relaxed by leaning against the tent porch and idly grasping at a bit of dangling cord while staring them out. Unfortunately, my lack of spatial awareness meant I fumbled and groped the air repeatedly, which made me look not cool but even more like the disgusting pants-destroying freak I already was.

I was still thinking of the perfect comeback when they walked away laughing, my reputation as a weird skank solidly in place for the rest of the trip and most probably the rest of school.

During the trip, Erin, who even with her low IQ was canny enough to realize my presence was social leprosy, took to ignoring me completely. In her absence I made friends with a scary girl by employing my knowledge of random facts to impress her.

'In France the legal drinking age is 14.'

Within half an hour we'd broken off from the school group. We got hammered on vodka and strawberry because in my excitement I couldn't remember the French for vodka and orange. When we returned to the group, I loudly declared everyone in our year to be Massive Bitches. I was so low status no one even turned around to look.

The only issue with my new friend was that she lied to me for her own entertainment, knowing that I'd believe absolutely anything people said so long as they said it with a straight face.

'Philip fancies you.'

'He does?' I felt hopeful. Nobody fancied me as no one wanted a girlfriend with a moustache and glasses but I felt glad at least one person in the school might have seen past all that.

She laughed. 'Yeah. He says you're soooooo fine!'

She clutched her sides laughing while I smiled to mirror her, uncertain what I was meant to find funny. Something felt odd here, especially as Philip never made eye contact with me or registered my presence in class at all. I felt uncomfortable but no one else would talk to me.

On the final night of the trip, I was sitting alone watching the disco they'd put on for us. Every single day, everyone had mentioned that I shat myself; and every night my bed had been filled with crushed-up crisps, bits of old rubbish and half-eaten sandwiches. And then something weird happened. I looked around at everyone and suddenly realized, with something far beyond a 14-year-old's perspective, that this social order, this hierarchy . . . None of this was permanent and everything would be okay. A sense of absolute peace came over me. I laughed a little in disbelief at the switch in my brain. It was like I'd zoomed out of being a teenager and been given an objective view of the rest of our lives. The sense of peace stayed with me for the rest of the trip and as girls glared and muttered about me when we boarded the bus home.

'DONALD FINGERED YOU!'

I was walking home from the bus stop with another girl when some boys from the Protestant school passed by. I vaguely knew the heckler, Fraser, as his sister played in the same piano competitions as me. I spun round to look at him.

'Yeah? So what?' I tilted my head back so I could look down my nose at him.

'Donald fingered you!' he repeated – the statement serving as fact, sentencing and judgement.

The term 'slut-shaming' hadn't been invented yet (and if it had, there's no way it would have made its way to Bathgate). I felt enraged and wanted to tell him and everyone else watching this post-school minidrama, 'Whatever you're doing, it doesn't work on me,' but he just kept repeating it. The girl I walked home from school with was a goody two-shoes who had definitely never been fingered; and like an olde worlde Southern gent I wanted to protect her ears from this. I turned away from him again as he was still shouting it gleefully like a maniac and engaging with him like a reasonable adult was doing nothing. Out of the corner of my eye I watched him arch his back and bellow it up into the sky then double over laughing.

'DONALD FINGERRRRRED YOUUUUUUUUU!'

'What's he talking about?' said my companion.

'Ignore it,' I said through gritted teeth.

I said bye to her and decided to visit my friend Elsie, who lived on our street but went to the Protestant school. Elsie was geeky and thoughtful and showed me films about Oscar Wilde and secretly gay Victorians. I'd sleep over at hers every Saturday and every Sunday we'd have pain au chocolat in bed and talk about books. Today, though, she wouldn't let me in the house and when she spoke her voice was shaky.

'I don't want to be your friend anymore. Every time I have a friend who's a boy you start going out with him.'

I didn't understand. She'd gone out with one of my brothers last summer and I hadn't kicked off about that. At least I understood there weren't many boys living on our hill and beggars couldn't be choosers. Some of us had to be fingered by moon-faced Protestants called Donald.

'You . . . *did it* with Donald and now you're doing it with Adam.'

I was dating her other friend, a sweet eccentric called Adam who had a pet rock called Leonard and was as much of a social pariah as I was. It wasn't like she'd said she fancied him or I'd stolen him off her. I didn't understand it. I still don't. Unsure of how to fix things and wary of confrontation, I shrugged, letting her shut the door on me. I trudged up the hill to my house and never saw her again.

I'd thought Elsie was a safe friend, one of the losers like me who didn't have secret rules or the frightening unpredictable cruelty of most girls at school. We had met when we were 12 but we were 14 now and at some point – overnight or when I wasn't looking at her – she had committed to the same secret code as all the other women-to-be and was now as distant and unreachable as the rest of them.

Later, when I first read about the pick-me trope[*] at university, I nodded in agreement. I thought there were definitely women like that, who failed to realize that men

---

[*]   A pick-me girl surrounds herself with boys to get validation, has mostly male friends and often insists she's 'not like other girls'.

would never stand up for them when it came to any kind of fight for gender equality. This thought was quickly followed by horror as I totted up every feature that matched me. *I* had a lot of male friends. *I* said I wasn't like other girls – and if I didn't say it, I was always thinking it. But I was never saying it to show I was better than other women. All I wanted was to find out how to be like other girls and it felt increasingly impossible. The pick-me girl appears to me as just another way to dismiss female autistics.

Out of anyone I know, I probably have the most positive virginity-loss story that still managed to end in negativity. I got rid of mine at 15 on a family holiday with a 19-year-old Mexican waiter called Gabriel who had a cracking body. I had a very unfortunate-looking boyfriend back home in Scotland who I felt nothing for but was dating because it seemed to be the done thing and because he'd silently handed me a poster of my favourite band when we went to Laser Quest in Falkirk. We kissed stiffly in the school playground, echoing the baby-couples around us in identical poses with their hands placed gingerly on each other's waists while other kids whooped and teachers tutted. It felt boring and gross but I guessed I had to get used to it as everyone was ugly at that school.

When Gabriel kissed me I felt a mad headrush followed by a heat in my stomach. I wondered if this was the feeling of love people banged on about. But it didn't make sense as

Gabriel spoke about four words of English and I thought you were supposed to know someone's hopes and dreams to fall in love with them. All I knew about Gabriel's hopes was that he was planning to go to America and join the Backstreet Boys and he was aiming to get a condom for us soon.

I attended the hotel's Spanish class so I could communicate with him as currently we were only able to communicate through the language of lust. Unfortunately, the class didn't offer actual practical phrases like, 'Do you have a condom?' so when it finished I furtively searched through a dictionary left on the table. *'Preservativo!'* I whispered to myself triumphantly.

After a lot of pleading with my parents to let me just chastely explore Cancún with a local, Gabriel and I rode off on a scooter to a motel and had sex. The mutual lack of fluency in each other's languages meant there was mercifully little small talk to navigate afterwards.

'It's uh-mazing. Basically, everyone is lying to us about sex,' I bragged to Erin on the phone.

Everyone said sex hurt and would be bad the first time unless you loved someone, in which case your clit would be magically stimulated and you'd have multiple orgasms all from the power of luuuuuurve. I felt like I was viewing the world with a degree of suspicion I hadn't had before – if everyone was lying about this, what else were they lying about? In the early 2000s, girls' magazines' main message about sex was to warn of the consequences of getting pregnant. I'd rather die than be pregnant so as soon as I got home I went to the doctor for contraceptives and condoms.

I addressed the GP briskly, woman to woman, which must have looked odd given I was a gangly teenager.

'I've been researching my options and I would like the contraceptive injection please. Not the pill; I've read research that says the pill is bad for you. Thank you.'

The doctor studied me weirdly. 'Is everything okay at home?' she asked.

'Yeah . . .'

'Are you sure?'

I couldn't understand why she was asking this, but fat tears plopped down my cheeks anyway – and like most tears they took me by surprise. Nothing in particular at home was wrong other than everything being as wrong as it always had been: there was the constant knowledge that my family didn't like me and everything I did led to them disliking me more. Other than that, everything was fine. Realistically, the doctor likely spotted my autism – my odd manner of speaking, weird eye contact and sexual precociousness – and misinterpreted this as something being 'up', but something she couldn't quite put her finger on.

'Okay, love,' she said softly. 'We'll put an implant in your arm but make sure to hide it from Mum and Dad.' I cried more, wanting her to help me but not for sex things; just to help me in general. It felt like she'd seen something and I was crying because I knew there was something wrong too, but I didn't have a word for it.

I came home from school one day to find Mum red-eyed. Not one for privacy, she'd raided through my things and found: 1) my diary bragging about what an amazing shagger

I was; and 2) a dangerous little collection of cards in my jacket pocket. The first was a C-Card,* then there was a little plastic card notifying the reader that I had a contraceptive implant in my left arm for the next three years, and then an appointment card from the sexual-health clinic.

She asked me, 'Why? Why did you do it?' over and over while I looked at her blankly.

'He was really fit,' I offered, truthfully. People said you should always tell the truth.

She sobbed harder. 'You could have just *kissed* him!'

Jeez. Sometimes it felt like we were characters in wildly different novels: Mum a wide-eyed schoolgirl in an Enid Blyton story and me a city slicker in a Jackie Collins bonkbuster. I shook my head no, thinking I couldn't tell someone like her about bodies being on fire and getting wet and hot lust.

'I really couldn't,' I said and then it was my turn to make a meaningful face and hope she'd know what I was on about.

'Is it self-esteem?' she asked. 'Peer pressure?' *As if* I'd copy anything those losers at school would do. I was having sex 'cause I'd got the horn and to a lesser extent I felt comfortable as my true peers – the characters in novels – did it and approved of it. The self-esteem thing had always baffled me as it had no basis in logic and I was driven primarily by logic and reason. Everyone around me said not having sex was a sign of a confident young woman

---

* The C-Card scheme gave young people access to free condoms: you showed your card at various health centres or youth centres and could fill your pockets and schoolbag with them – a great idea given that Catholic schools in Scotland like to pretend teenagers don't have sex.

who respected herself. But if that were true then why were all the shy kids at school still virgins? I thought of Zoe Watts, a specky diabetic who peed herself in French class after they wouldn't let her out. No one ever said about her: 'Zoe's got low self-esteem; she had a threeway round the back of the school bins.'*

Mum had also found I wasn't eating my school lunches. I wasn't eating them because the noise and crowd and lights in school were stressing me out. Bizarrely, I ended up looking forward to the hellishly stressful experience of being in school, as it meant I could avoid coming home to Mum crying in her bedroom every day. It made me angry when she cried. It felt manipulative.

While I can only speak for myself, I believe there's a significant number of autistic women who have sex freely because we've little regard for gender norms or complex social hierarchies (for example, promiscuity carries a heavy social cost as a woman) and it's sensorily enjoyable. This is something not often considered as people are uncomfortable thinking of autistics as sexual creatures, plus society is still remarkably inept at taking female sexual agency into consideration at all.

On the second day of tears Mum started up with 'What would your grandparents say?' – the chorus to her classic hit 'Why did you do this?' I reflected on the inappropriateness of Mum telling Gran I'd fucked a Mexican waiter. Her call, I

---

*   Frustratingly, psychologist and autism expert Tony Attwood and other writers of female-specific autism literature put forward the self-esteem myth a lot. In one lecture Attwood claims that autistic girls may become promiscuous to get peer approval.

guessed. I told her she could do that if she liked but it felt like an odd dinner-table topic.

'I warned you about getting in trouble,' Mum blubbed on the third day of endless crying.

I considered this baffling statement for a moment as I stared miserably at my feet. In the absence of any sex education, I had responsibly taken it upon myself to go get contraceptives. I'd just got another load of As at school. From what I could see I was fitting all the criteria of being a 'good girl'.

While Mum cried I worked hard to zone out of the room and have a think. For ages she had been taking me aside and saying in a weird tone of voice, 'You don't want to get in *trouble* now, do you?'

I'd shake my head no and work harder at school. It seemed an odd thing to say. I never got in any serious trouble and my status as one of the well-behaved ones in class was firmly established. Now I looked at her crying and it dawned on me she was using 'trouble' as a code word for 'shagging'. I felt furious at her. Why didn't she just *say* that, then? Why did everyone go around speaking in code then getting angry at me because I didn't have the glossary for their secret language? And how was something as nice as sex 'trouble' anyway?

I decided there and then I must be adopted. It all added up. I'd never seen my birth certificate and it didn't seem possible that I was related to these people with their odd ways. It felt too much like I'd been dropped in from somewhere else. I would go on to believe I was adopted well into adulthood, until they finally showed me my birth certificate.

*

I managed to get a Saturday job in Boots. There was another girl there my age but she was nothing like me. Her existence seemed purely emblematic of how crap my impression of a normal girl was. Neat little Amanda, a mini-fishwife who slotted in with all the other fishwives. She had a man and she couldn't wait to marry him. The older women in the shop, Jean and Carolyn, adored her. Jean was the nicer of the two, with a dry sense of humour and some sympathy towards the fact that I was utterly socially incompetent. Carolyn used to be pretty but wasn't any more and seemed fucking furious about it. Predictably, she hated me on sight.

'What's the new No7 mascara like?' a customer asked.

I was wearing a large badge that read: 'ASK ME ABOUT THE NEW NO7 MASCARA!'

'Awful. Terrible. It's so cheap; the formula doesn't go on easily at all. Try the L'Oréal one instead.'

My boss's eyes bulged in the background. As soon as the woman was out the door and out of earshot she scurried over.

'You can't say that.'

'But the badge says to ask me about the new mascara.'

'Yes, but you've just said it's terrible.'

I looked at her helplessly. She didn't seem to realize that if I was meant to lie and say it was good, I'd need another badge pinned to my eyeballs instructing me to do so. Ideally, everyone would wear badges telling me exactly what to say in this hellscape as seemingly I could say nothing that wasn't wrong or offensive in some way.

On the weekend before Christmas we were asked to come in to work in fancy dress. Everyone arrived wearing delicate little reindeer antlers, Santa hats or tiny sparkly fairy wings. I turned up in 5-foot fairy wings that spanned my back and had to spend the day apologizing for knocking stock off the corners of every shelf while Carolyn and Jean glowered at me.

Every Saturday at home I'd do a little stand-up routine at the dining-room table on how awful it was to work there and my parents would cry laughing at my impressions of Jean and Carolyn, wiping the tears away as I retold every insult I'd saved up in my head that day. I didn't feel close to my parents in any other way, so it was striking how good it felt to make them laugh; it almost made the awfulness worth it. I edited out the bits where my manager moved me to work by myself in the stock room as I was such a liability, and completely omitted the fact I was now shoplifting prolifically.

Fifth year should have been incredible. It should have been my year. All the girls who'd hit me with a hockey stick in PE or called me a lesbo had left to do the only two jobs open to girls at our school – hairdressing or childcare – and I could stop studying subjects that were deeply irrelevant to me, like religious education or woodwork or maths.

'I don't need maths.'

'You can't just do languages.'

'Why not?'

Our assistant head – a maths teacher, coincidentally – glared at me. I was irritating to him in a way that he hadn't come across before, as what I was doing didn't involve setting fire to stuff or smashing people's heads on desks.

'You will need maths later in life and taking Higher maths is compulsory in this school.'

'I only want to study English and languages because I only like those subjects.'

My mum sat by me, a steadfast negotiator.

'I think Fern mentioned doing music as a fifth subject as she's good at piano?' she offered.

'She can't do that; it doesn't fit in her timetable.'

He sat back, his jaw tense. Mum didn't budge. Then he sighed, defeated. He didn't have time for this: there were bin fires to be put out and sectarian jokes to be made.

'Fine. You'll do four Highers and can have a free hour to use each week for studying. And you *will* use it for study.'

I'll study so much it'll shock you, dickhead.

I smiled at him.

I was the only fifth year given a special studying hour. Normally only the sixth form had free periods. This was how I met Lauren. Lauren was one of the most popular girls in the year above me – but not in the way most popular girls were popular. People loved her because she was funny and had an ability to roast teachers with the comic timing of an old pro. I was sitting studying alone in the dinner hall when she and a couple of girls approached my table.

'Anyone sitting here?'

I side-eyed them, hunched over my books. She'd tried to talk to me at a party the other week but I never knew anymore if girls were taking the piss out of me or genuinely wanted to be my friend so I'd opted to ignore her.

'No.'

Lauren took a copy of *Heat* and started flicking through it, commenting on it to the girls that were with her. I mentally rolled my eyes at her. People who took an interest in celebrities were morons. I was a refined intellectual, absorbed in my novels and pursuit of knowledge.

'Wow, her tits are up to her ears, eh?'

She looked at me sidelong, trying to catch my eye as I pretended to read.

'What do you think, Fern?'

I sighed in irritation and shrugged. 'Dunno.'

'I wish I had wee tits like Paris Hilton. Mine are so big I have to hold onto them when I'm getting in the bath.'

I started laughing and reluctantly stopped studying.

From then on in, I was always with her. Being friends with her meant I could sit with the other girls instead of in the toilet cubicles at lunch. I didn't have to talk too much. She seemed to think I was interesting, wasn't bitchy in an underhand way and had social intuition; she knew how to just *be* around all kinds of people in a way that seemed so effortless as to appear magical to me.

We were in the library laughing with a group of girls one day. I was feeling almost normal for the first time since primary school when Lauren said mildly, 'You fidget a lot.'

'Do I?' I looked down at my hands for the first time and noticed they were moving of their own accord. I banished them under the table, where they could flicker and fidget and dance about without bothering anyone.

Lauren nudged me then, whispering: 'You ever noticed when a guy comes over to a table of girls, the girls stop being funny and start laughing at everything the guy is saying instead?'

I nodded.

On cue, the table of girls we were sat at (who'd previously all been raucous and funny in their own right) tee-heed delicately in unison, suddenly in thrall to some ugly-but-hot-for-our-school guy. Lauren's gayness and my autism meant we both had a distaste for so-called 'normal' social dynamics.

Chapter Four

'I am an architect,
They call me a butcher,
I am a pioneer,
They call me primitive,
I am purity,
They call me perverted'

—Manic Street Preachers, 'Faster'

I managed four years at secondary school before I started walking out without a word of explanation. Out of the classroom, through the car park, out the school gates. No one followed me. It felt miraculous – I was 15 and had been so attached to following rules my entire life that it hadn't occurred to me that there would be absolutely no consequence to breaking them.

My school was in a different village to my home town and the only person I knew there was my grandfather so I decided to walk to his house. For many kids, this would have been a pleasant way to spend an afternoon off school, were it not for the fact my granda was a 20-stone alcoholic who I felt no fondness for or attachment to.

Still, my options on where to go to avoid getting caught were limited and Granda's lack of working memory was a serious advantage. He'd recently been diagnosed with a thing called Korsakoff's syndrome, brought on by his decades-long commitment to prodigious binge drinking, and it had led to lesions forming on his brain. He had been given his own social worker but she'd refused to work with him after he kept forgetting to wear trousers or pants when he answered the door. He used to embarrass us by telling the police our address when he drunkenly collapsed in the street. One time the kids at school found out he was related to me and I remember the surprise on their faces, that the geeky kid was related to the village drunk. They'd shaken their heads in disbelief when I nodded in response to them asking, 'That guy's your granda? *That guy?* Seriously?'

For years I'd pass pubs and wonder why they smelled of Granda's house: a mix of whisky, stale sweat and musty furniture. It took me ages to realize that Granda smelled like a pub, not that all pubs smelled of Granda.

Granda accepted my visit without a smile or any sign of recognition. I could've been anyone. He eyed me sidelong from the armchair. I plonked down on the couch with a tea I'd made myself and looked at the ugly green porcelain toad where Granda's glasses sat, permanently out of action as he had been too drunk for years now to focus on anything but the telly.

I didn't say anything. Granda looked ruefully at his empty whisky glass. The room stank of whisky along with a sour, pickled smell I couldn't put my finger on.

'Where's Kathleen?'

'She went to Ireland, remember?'

'Oh aye.' His eyes swivelled back to the horses on the screen.

For as long as I could remember Toodaloo had been going on holiday to the island we were originally from in Donegal to see her 'best friend' Hugh. The holidays had gotten longer and longer and her visits back to her and Granda's house were just that – visits. No one in the family really acknowledged she'd stealth-dumped Granda.

'How can she call herself a Catholic when she wants a divorce?'

'Eh, dunno.'

'She shouldnae be allowed in a church.'

Everyone in the family seemed to call Granda by his first name, Drew, even his own kids. I assumed this was to demonstrate our collective dislike of him so was surprised when one of my aunts bought him a budgie to keep him company.

'Drew gets lonely,' she'd assured us. To the rest of us this was a madness – it didn't matter whether it was animals or humans, Granda despised the company of other living creatures.

'Where's Larsson?' I said now, nodding to the empty cage. The budgie had been named after the Swedish Celtic striker Henrik Larsson.

He glanced at the cage blankly. 'Gone. Oot the door.'

'What do you mean?'

'I opened the cage and he flew oot the front door.'

'Oh. Oh no. Well. Maybe he'll come back?'

'Naw. He's gone now.'

One eye seemed to swivel towards me without the other one moving. Granda had big, bulging eyes set at opposite ends of his head like a fish. I remembered Dad mentioning they'd been removed and popped back in during surgery and had never looked right since.

'By god, yer a fine-looking lassie.'

'It's me, Granda. It's Fern. Paul's daughter?'

A flicker of recognition. 'Paul? That bastard . . .'

I tried to laugh but the silence was excruciating. I'd never really chatted to Granda before – usually he was so drunk we just piled cushions and ornaments on him and played human Buckaroo. I stared at the racehorses on TV, trying and failing to think of something to say to the guy. Like the needle on a record returning to the first song, Granda's brain whirred, clicked and reset.

'By god, yer a fine-looking lassie.'

'Yeah. It's Fern, Paul's daughter.'

'Oh right. Right. Sorry. Aye. How's he getting on, the fucking bastard? Heh heh heh.'

I looked at my watch. Only another hour then I could go home without raising suspicion.

'By god, yer a fine-looking lassie . . .'

When I got home that afternoon, Mum was in hysterics because she'd found out I'd been cutting myself. Personally, I was more upset because I felt I had no ownership over my life and now it seemed like I had no ownership over my body either. The spells of her crying over something I'd done were becoming more frequent, whether it was me not eating my packed lunch (an afternoon of crying) or having sex (a whole week of crying) and now this. I didn't like it when Mum cried; not because I felt guilt or shame but because I found other people crying incredibly uncomfortable. It seemed to demand an equally explosive emotional response that I just didn't have. Instead, I'd make myself stay as still as possible and not look at the crier until they'd regained composure. My memories of others crying have no faces – only the image of a toaster, a bookshelf, a wall.

It was already hard to be in school with the itchy blazer, the fluorescent lighting burning my eyes, the constant noise and the bitchy cliques. I'd just about coped with all that but what had driven me over the edge was a self-imposed pressure to ace my exams that started a full year before I even sat my Highers.

I knew from the novels I read that being the best at school was key to escaping my house and leaving Bathgate altogether. When I expressed my worries over failing exams, some adults spouted mealy-mouthed platitudes like, 'There are different types of intelligence'; but when you quizzed them, those people had always done crap at school so I was hardly going to listen to them. My rigid, binary thinking decided there were clever people and there were stupid people and in exams there was only succeeding or failing. The exam boards awarded you an A, B or C; there was no grade called 'Well, we all have different positive qualities'. I decided if I didn't get three As I'd kill myself at the end of the school year. There was no other option.

'This!' Mum screamed, tearing at the ragged-edged magazine pictures on my bedroom wall. 'This is why you do it!' I'd Blu Tacked a photo from *NME* of the Manic Street Preachers' guitarist Richey Edwards carving '4REAL' into his arm. Mum's theory that I'd simply seen pictures and copied them – rather than accepting that I felt depressed and sought out reflections of that in the culture around me – was such an asinine line of thinking that I didn't bother challenging it. I was too tired anyway. Instead, I silently watched as more posters were ripped off my walls.

Often during these fights I was unable to say or do much but I could feel the badness prickling my chest and building up inside me, climbing up my throat until the pressure ballooned in my head and made it hard to breathe. It didn't seem physically possible, that the poison could continue to build up over this many years without my head exploding and splattering up the wall like one of those YouTube videos where they attach elastic bands to a watermelon.

Usually after the shouting she'd sit crying and plead with me: 'Why are you doing this to yourself? Don't you know you'll have scars? Why would you want to do that?'

Again, her line of thinking was so back to front. I couldn't find a polite way to express that I found living with my family torture. Living in a noisy house with four other people would be tricky for any autistic but for one still undiagnosed, trying to manage the sensory overwhelm from school combined with normal exam pressure, a breakdown was inevitable.

The only fail of my cutting era was the time I ambitiously carved 'FUCK!' into my leg. I couldn't keep up the depth and precision for all the letters meaning they healed at different speeds and consequently I spent two weeks with the much cheerier 'A-OK!' taunting me every time I got undressed.

I really liked my friends at school that year – a mix of boys and girls all into the same music and going to skateparks and gigs. I couldn't work out why I was making excuses not to meet them at lunch. Instead, I'd go and sit alone in the library with my head in my hands. Thinking about exams and success and whether or not I would have to kill myself all day and all night was exhausting and meant the prospect of following a group conversation in a lunch hall of 400 kids was suddenly too much. Increasingly I was needing the hour alone at lunch just to buy myself enough energy to act normal in class. Soon, even that stopped working – which was why I'd started walking out of school completely to go sit in Granda's house.

I didn't want to freak out our family GP by telling him everything, like how I had to rock in my rocking chair for hours after school or punch the walls to get to sleep at night or about cutting 'A-OK!' into my leg. The way I saw it, I said, feigning as much calm as possible, I just needed people to stop moving or touching my stuff in the house. The only diagnosis I could find that vaguely lined up with this was OCD, but just talking to doctors was impossible as I was unable to articulate the full extent of my problems – essentially I was fumbling in the dark to describe what I didn't know. I couldn't tell him that all the noise my family made drove me nuts and that the smell of the washing powder in supermarkets made me want to cry and that I had to hit things just to calm down.

Instead, I said: 'I've always felt strange. Even before this. Maybe it's OCD.' I saw him write, 'Says she's always been strange. Thinks it's OCD.'

I was sent off with a prescription for Prozac and took it obediently. Within a month I was crazier than ever and it made me cut deeper and more often. With hindsight this isn't surprising at all, given I was on a dose intended for an allistic person when I should have been on either a lower dose or no medication at all.

The autistic scientist Temple Grandin has pointed out that autistic people frequently require much lower doses of antidepressants than non-autistic people do. Her argument is that our nervous systems are so sensitive that we need less of everything – alcohol, recreational drugs, caffeine – for it to have an impact. Too high a dose of antidepressants, Grandin states, 'will result in agitation, insomnia, aggression, and excitement.'* However, this is not true of all autistic people and some might find higher doses of such drugs helpful. The main point here is that the ways in which medications affect autistic people are extremely under-researched and poorly understood and many of us suffer as a consequence. I know I did.

I was rapidly running out of cutting real estate on my arms and legs so I went back to the GP. They doubled my dose of Prozac. When my parents hid the razors, I got a tiny screwdriver from the cupboard where they kept the tools and retreated back to my room. I dug out my pencil case, unscrewed and removed

---

* Grandin, T (2006) *Thinking in Pictures and Other Reports from My Life with Autism*. Vintage.

the blade from my pencil sharpener and defiantly cut myself with that instead. It was a nice challenge.

I took an overdose not long after that.

I remember my parents' baffled surprise when they came to pick me up at A&E and a couple of days later I found myself sitting in front of a hospital psychiatrist.

'I can't . . . I don't know how to explain it, really . . . It's too much.'

The word 'Herculean' flashed on and off like a neon light in my head. *A Herculean effort*. It was taking a Herculean effort to seem normal. I should tell her that. Be articulate. But when it came to it nothing was coming out the way I wanted.

'It's like a – it's like a Herculean effort to . . .' I trailed off, grasping for a way to describe what I was feeling.

The psychiatrist looked at me. She was young and blonde and panicked.

'I . . . I think there's a place that may be able to help you. Do you want me to arrange a visit? I can check if they have space?'

I was stunned. Something was happening. Help was coming, maybe.

'Yes. Please.' I didn't even hesitate.

She made a phone call and within days my parents and I pulled up to a place that looked like a rectangular block of battered '80s council flats. I strained my head to try and see a hospital building. There were no indications of a hospital setting. Just a beige and red brick residential block. We walked up to a bright yellow door and were buzzed in.

As we reached the top of the stairs there was a big whiteboard that had 'AM' and 'PM' scrawled on it at the top.

Underneath were various names, indicating who was attending that day:

LAURA, NATALIE, KEVIN (Weds only), ANNA

A slender, glamorous woman with long highlighted hair welcomed us in.

'I'm Lorraine, and there's only two things I dislike and that's poor timekeeping and Hibs losing.' She chuckled at her own joke. *Oh god*. She was one of *them*. The authority figure that wanted to be seen as cool and down with the kids. I just wanted a medical professional to give me therapy and tell me why I suddenly couldn't function in school and felt as though the world was caving in. Instead, I got dumb football jokes.

My parents laughed uncomfortably. Dad looked quietly horrified by the whole thing, like he was trying his very best to mentally transport himself out of this place.

'This is our classroom . . .'

A small girl with short hair and loads of tattoos sat at a computer with her back to us. She turned around to look at us. She had huge mischievous eyes and grinned at me.

'Hiya.'

'Hiya, I'm Fern.'

'I'm Natalie.'

'What are you studying for?'

'Standard Grade maths and Standard Grade English.'

I waited for her to list more but that was it. Two Standard Grades.

'I'm doing Higher English, French, Italian and Modern Studies.'

'No maths, naw?'

I shook my head shyly. 'Nah. Maths is crap anyway and—'

'Ah-ah-ah!' Suddenly, Lorraine's finger wagged in my face. I shrunk back from the finger in surprise. 'Crap is *not* a Westleigh Way word.'

I felt my lip curl in disgust. She couldn't be serious. This was like a hack scene in a film about psych wards.

'But . . . crap isn't a swear word?'

I clocked my parents, already nodding at her approvingly.

Lorraine smiled at me with only her mouth. Her eyes said: 'Good luck proving me wrong, ya cow.' I decided there and then that I hated her. She repeated her slogan again smoothly: 'It's just *not* a Westleigh Way word.'

'But it's—'

'Fern—' one of my parents cautioned sharply.

As Lorraine showed us out, my mum schmoozing with her all the way down the stairs, I was reeling, trying to make sense of how it could be possible that in school I was firmly established as top of the class: straight-A student, brainy, used big words; weird, yes, but not a rule-breaker. A new identity had been abruptly assigned to me overnight, one where my speech was to be monitored and where I was to be spoken to like a particularly slow child. I followed my parents down the stairs and back out the building in silence.

As soon as our car doors thumped shut, I laughed bitterly.

' "Crap is *not* a Westleigh Way word," ' I said in my best patronizing Lorraine voice before shaking my head. 'I mean, who talks like that? It was like *One Flew Over the Cuckoo's Nest* or something, eh?'

Neither of them turned around. My mum's head turned slightly towards my dad, who still looked thoroughly distressed by the whole thing. In the tradition of Irish Catholics everywhere, my dad has always done his best to completely ignore any and all mental illness. To do that while being taken on a tour of an actual psychiatric unit was challenging, but I had to hand it to him: he'd made a solid effort.

'I think it'll teach her discipline,' Mum said coldly.

I gripped the back of her seat.

'*What*? What are you talking about, discipline? I don't *need* discipline!' I was doing my homework on the bus home from school and French verb drills for hours at a time each night. The whole reason I'd got myself into this state was obsessing over the perfect grades that'd get me into the perfect university and set me on the path to my perfect life.

Dad cleared his throat and nodded to Mum, still desperate to do and say as little as possible.

'Aye.'

I tried to sound calm. 'But I don't need to go in there. It's not even a swear word! I was just making conversation with that girl!'

Silence. Dad cleared his throat and started the car. I tried to stay quiet but couldn't.

'You do know it's not for discipline, eh? Like, it's a mental unit.'

I wasn't sure how they'd got mental illness conflated with me having done something wrong but there didn't seem to be any chance of reasoning with them now.

'You're going,' Mum said, sounding oddly satisfied.

I stared hard into the back of her daft curly head. Bitch. And him, Pontius Pilate, going along with anything she said so he could wash his hands of it. Pathetic.

I will never ever forgive you for this. I will hold this over you forever. You will think I'll forget and realize you're right, but I won't ever forgive you.

By that evening I'd reconciled myself to my new fate. It was obviously going to be ridiculous and ineffective. I'd use it as an experience. I'd imagine I was in a film about mental units. I'd pretend I was in a book.

On Monday a black cab arrived outside the house to take me there. As far as my friends at school were concerned, I was on study leave. I was amazed you could just disappear from school and no one questioned it. On reflection, though, this happened fairly often to girls at school. They had babies or breakdowns then one day they weren't there. Beyond a few whispers they might as well have never existed.

Lorraine was the head nurse and below her were two older women who as far as I could tell had zero qualifications or purpose other than to patronize and antagonize us at every opportunity. There was Lizzie, a skinny, dazed-looking woman with art-teacher vibes who was our occupational therapist. Lizzie talked like she was constantly spaced out – and given she was visibly suffering from an eating disorder it riled me to be lectured by her on recovery while she took 15 minutes to eat four carrot sticks at lunch.

Then there was our teacher, Mr Carr. One teacher among maybe eight of us, all at wildly different educational levels. Only two of us were doing Highers: me and Craig, who was only in once a week. I liked Mr Carr a lot better than the tightly wound, clenched-jawed teachers in my normal school, who all seemed to be on the verge of breakdowns themselves and taking it out on us. Contrastingly, Mr Carr had a dazed quality to him that really fitted the sense that we were all on a minibreak from life.

They didn't call us 'patients' even though that's blatantly what we were. They called us 'the young people'. For reasons I couldn't put my finger on at the time, I found this maddening. Like elsewhere in our lives, the approved terminology there seemed designed to ignore what was happening – because everyone found it distasteful to say we were in there for being mentally ill. I'm sure there were loads of HR meetings higher up in the local authority or at government level on how to label us, but it all felt so stupidly performative.

There were only two boys among us. Craig was the same age as me and I guessed had OCD and some generalized anxiety. Craig constantly looked nervy and jumpy but just came into class, did his revision and went home again. He never had to come to group therapy or do 'feeling drawings' with us or sit and eat stupid amounts of hospital food at lunch.

Then there was Kevin. Kevin had a scarf wrapped permanently around the lower half of his face and almost never spoke; and even when he did, it was never more than one or two words. Disfigurement or no, only two men to that many women made them hot to us. This was a problem. Craig's madness was too nervy to be appealing and Kevin was too young for me. Besides, I didn't want to find out what was or wasn't under the scarf.

The other option was lezzing off with each other, which, from what I gathered from the heavy innuendo during our smoke breaks, had happened loads.

Among the girls was Sadie, a veteran of these places and the leader of our group. Sadie was short, her face pitted with acne, and looked about 40. 'I've been trying to kill myself since I was eight,' she explained as we queued for thick, gluey pasta bake at lunch. I nodded sympathetically. She sighed, stacking garlic bread on top of a wodge of macaroni. 'One day I'll manage.' She said this in the same way that you tell a new colleague that you're aiming to move teams or get a promotion. Sadie was 13 but her world-weariness gave her a hefty authority.

Westleigh Way was in a rundown area that was seemingly made up of nothing but hospitals and roundabouts, so most lunchtimes we'd all wander up to the grim local shopping centre and wander back. On the walk there, there was a lamp post bent over at a 45-degree angle. Every day, Sadie would look at it jutting out the concrete and say, 'One day that lamp post's gonna fall on me and it's gonna kill me' – and every day, one of us would say, 'Not today, though.' She'd stare off into the distance, tensing her jaw determinedly. 'No. But one day.'

Ellie had blonde hair cut in a precise bob and was a total mystery to me. She never said anything about why she was there, never said anything odd and, crucially, never once referred to the fact we were all in a mental unit (the rest of us joked about it all the time). Sometimes when she spoke she sounded sad but

I waited and waited for Ellie to do or say something weird and she never broke. She was 14.

Laura was also 14 and had been at the same school I transferred to after I left Westleigh Way. Later, I found out at my new school that her best friend had moved away so Laura stopped speaking and they put her in there. She was a goth. She had dyed-black hair, purple lipstick and eye makeup but always wore a terrified puppyish expression. Even though she rarely made eye contact and shook her head resolutely whenever staff tried to trick her into talking, I liked her immediately. I made it my mission to get Laura to talk.

Then there was Natalie, the tattooed girl I'd met on the first day. Looking at her arms, a lot of the tattoos looked like a DIY effort, so I figured they had something to do with why she was in there, and from what I gathered from my brief time in group therapy she was groomed by an older man and raped. Her numerous tattoos were her response.

Every day, we'd have a cup of tea and biscuits on arrival. Then group therapy, art therapy, the tiniest bit of school, lunch time, leisure time. Afternoon was one-on-one therapy then we went home early, much earlier than on a normal school day. It took me less than a week of this meandering lazy routine to get worried.

'Stop reading your Italian dictionary at lunch, Fern.'

I looked up. It was my least favourite of the two old women tutting over me. 'But I'm studying. I have Highers.'

It took all my willpower not to shout, 'I'm not doing one Standard Grade in woodwork like the rest of those planks; I've a university offer that's within spitting distance.'

'Have a break from studying. Eat your tag-lee-ah-telly – that's Italian food.'

'The correct Italian pronunciation is actually *tah-lia-telle*. The *g* is silent.'

Old Bitch pursed her lips in annoyance before pasting on a fake chirpy voice, 'Well, in here it's *tag-lee-ah-telly* and that's that.'

She slammed a side plate down. I didn't understand why everything there was a battle of wills.

'I'm just trying to help you pronounce it properly.'

I shrugged and went back to studying so I never had to be around these sorts of people again.

That afternoon as we glued pasta shells onto sheets of A4, I started to see my bright future in academia dissolving. Mustering all the calm that I could, I told them that my constant studying wasn't a mental illness thing but a university thing and they needed to give me more school time. To be on the safe side, I also told my parents about it that evening and for once their rigid discipline worked in my favour as I saw them exchange panicked looks. They must have mentioned it to the unit because the following day my routine changed from drawing, therapy and a tiny bit of school to: school, lunch, school, home.

Having a quiet place to revise and not feel overwhelmed by the need to pretend to be a normal teenager for eight hours a day was good enough for me. We had a new nurse start midway through my stay there: Sam, a smiley Glaswegian guy in his thirties. There were whispers that Sam had worked in Carstairs (where the real mad people were and where it was rumoured they'd once skinned a nurse alive) so we all looked at him in awe. I noticed on my way in one morning that there were two baby seats in the back of his car so later I politely asked if he had twins. The happy chatter of the staff eating lunch abruptly stopped. Sam froze and looked away from me and back to the staff. Cutlery clattered down on someone's plate. I looked to Lorraine, who had stopped in her tracks on her way to the table and was looking at Sam. I felt my anxiety rise rapidly and scrambled for something to say to fix it.

'I was just – I thought because of the car seats you . . . Didn't you say you'd had a baby?'

Sam didn't reply and looked at Lorraine. As if some silent pact had been made between them, Lorraine turned to me coldly and said in an odd voice I didn't recognize: 'You're not to ask personal questions and I think you know that—'

'But I was making small talk!'

She held up a hand to silence me. 'Mr Carr has reported you were asking personal questions in class too.'

'What?! What did I even—'

I had trusted Mr Carr implicitly and facing the fact that he was one of *them* was too painful to comprehend. I looked over at him for some kind of explanation, incredulous. He avoided my gaze, swallowing the last of his apple crumble. The betrayal sucked the air out my lungs.

'You know what you did. You asked him intrusive questions about previous schools he had taught at.'

I remembered then the pleasant, seemingly inconsequential exchange we'd had in class on a peaceful afternoon where I was the only one there.

'Which school did you teach at before?'

He had smiled at me.

'Bo'ness Academy.'

That was all that had been said. I looped the exchange over and over in my mind's eye, scouring my memory for signs that maybe I hadn't asked him a polite question and had in fact called him a wanker, but there was nothing. I started to explain in protest. Mr Carr would back me up, I offered; but before I could say anything more, Lorraine cut in.

'You know what you did wrong and I think you should go back to the school room now.'

My mouth opened and closed but I couldn't say or do anything other than shake my head at the sheer injustice of it all. I stormed upstairs to one of the disused bathrooms from when the building was still a residential unit and booted the bath. A lifetime of following rules meant I was terrified to show my temper anywhere outside of the house, so I restrained myself from kicking it as hard as I wanted. My rage felt too dangerous to be aired outside of my bedroom. As I kicked it, a sheet of plywood attached to the side of the bath fell off and thudded dustily on the floor. Frantically, I picked it up and tried to wedge it back in place so it looked how it did before. They'd absolutely *love* it if I destroyed their property. It seemed clear now that they'd been trying to find something on me for weeks.

'I was ASKING! POLITELY! ABOUT HIS *BABY*. I was being polite!'

Watching me shout in the safety of the smoking area, Sadie shook her head. She and Natalie exchanged knowing glances. Sadie patted me.

'He was in Carstairs, mind. They think everyone's gonna

kill their kid so they can't talk about them. They have different rules. You didn't do anything wrong.'

I've discovered that one of the most hurtful aspects of crossed wires in a lifetime of dealing with allistic people is that they tend to look for and assume there's an unspoken agenda in your behaviour. When they do that with autistic people – who are the least Machiavellian people on earth and not great at making speedy social calculations – they read our awkward attempts at small talk as cold and manipulative; they mistake our fact-finding questions for prying. Lots of autistic women find eye contact just as uncomfortable as autistic men do but our social camouflaging leads us to attempt it anyway and consequently some of us hold people's gaze for an unnervingly long amount of time. Couple all this with the tendency for society to assume that women in general are scheming and you have a toxic mix of mistrust and misunderstanding. People frequently took my sincerity as calculated in some way and my insincerity as truth.

It seems clear to me now that the staff were forming a picture of me as conniving and sinister and my polite attempts at small talk were my plotting to murder their children outside school hours.

Remember: this wasn't a borstal or a prison or even a residential ward. We were in there because we were depressed teens who were too hopeless or anxious to function within the mainstream school system.

I was tired of getting in trouble when I hadn't done anything wrong and after the Sam incident I gave up trying to do anything right. In the lunch queue we talked about self-harm as openly as others discuss the weather. I had run out of space on my arms that could be covered up with bangles or sleeves and my excuses were running out and delivered with little conviction. When my sleeves slid up during a piano lesson, I weakly told my teacher 'an angry cat attacked me'.

'I do it on my stomach and my legs,' Natalie whispered as we queued for hospital oven chips. 'They never find it there.'

'That's so cool,' I whispered back, genuinely impressed at the ingenuity. 'I've been running out of space on the top of my arms and I don't want to do it any further down in case people notice.'

Natalie shook her head slightly and gave me a warning look. I looked up and one of the Old Bitches had tipped off Lorraine, who was glaring at us with her arms folded. I looked back at her coldly. What, they were controlling my one release now? Was there any way we were allowed to express ourselves here?

There was occupational therapy. Occupational therapy was doing stuff like drawing a portrait of Natalie or Sadie with a sheet of paper over your hand and never checking what you were drawing so you could learn to *trust yourself*. As a skilled draughtswoman, I found this preposterous. Looking at our wonky drawings afterwards – the eyes about two feet apart from each other and Natalie's nose somewhere above her ears because I hadn't been allowed to look at the paper – I wondered if Lizzie made this shit up for a laugh. That or the lack of calories was starting to affect her brain. Sometimes I felt like we were just in a holding pen to make everyone outside – our families, teachers, healthcare providers – more comfortable.

Every day had the same reassuring routine with little change, although there was always something interesting happening in the shadows. Sadie and Ellie were giving each other conspiratorial looks when I arrived at breakfast one day but giggled and shook their heads when I asked them what was happening. During our mid-morning tea and biscuits, Sadie sidled up to me and slipped me an envelope, which I quickly stuffed in my pocket. Out the corner of her mouth she said, 'Natalie wants to meet you in the games room at lunch.'

I was confused. Before school started, I went and locked myself in the toilet upstairs and took the envelope out my pocket. There were two pieces of paper in it. One was a poem. One was something between a poem and a letter, I guess. There was a heaviness in the bottom of the envelope. I peeked in and pulled out a necklace, one of those lockets from the Elizabeth Duke at Argos range. It was a locket that was one half of a heart. I grimaced, putting it back in the envelope and pulling out the letter.

Who is the funniest girl in all of Westleigh Way?
Who tells the best stories and makes me laugh every day?
Who has the best eyes and looks great in her bandana?

I'd taken to wearing a stars-and-stripes bandana on my head. It looked deranged and truly only people in a psych unit would think otherwise.

I'll give ye one guess.
Have you guessed it yet haha? It's FERN.

I shivered involuntarily and looked at the other piece of paper. It was like an incantation.

> When I look into your eyes I see the sun setting on
> a deserted beach. I see palm trees. I see the ocean . . .

I was feeling a mix of things. Mainly overwhelming embarrassment. But it quickly occurred to me that I finally had an opportunity to get off with a girl who wasn't just one of my schoolfriends.

We went outside for a smoke. While we were finishing up I noticed there was an odd giggly tension because the others knew and I knew that they knew about the letters. I waited for them to start trudging back inside before turning to Natalie. I took a deep breath before trying to say it casually . . .

'D'you want to play pool at lunchtime?'

Natalie's eyes widened. I remembered watching a series called *Bad Girls* and figured I'd cracked some sort of prison lesbian code. She smiled. 'Eh . . . aye that'd be great.'

I went back to school, panicking and excitedly wondering what we'd even *do*. There was also a feeling of triumph, like, *If you're going to make me be here, I'll lez off. You can talk to us all like we're stupid but* you're *the dumb ones. Because of all the ways you thought we'd get in trouble in your heterosexist worldview, you can't conceive of the patients getting off with each other.*

During my English class, Mr Carr pottered about, smiling into the middle distance and doing nothing in particular. Evidently the guy loved it there; it was an absolute skive of a job. I smiled politely but kept chat as minimal as possible: I couldn't be too careful since the last attempt at basic small talk went awry. I looked at my revision notes, tap-tap-tapping my pen on the desk and looking at the clock to see when lunch was. At lunchtime I ate as little as I could get away with. The Old Bitches were petty and chastising in their usual way but I, saint-like, raised my eyes to heaven and smiled through it.

I climbed the two flights of stairs to the games room two at a time. Natalie was already in there wearing a baseball cap, a white vest top and a push-up bra. She was racking up at the pool table. I scrunched up my face in confusion. Maybe she actually *did* want to play pool? She turned to me and smiled.

'Do you want to break?'

I thought about what the others said, about 'pool' being a code.

'Natalie, I didn't . . . come here to play pool.' I cringed at the line but it was happening now so I walked up to her and took her baseball cap off to test the waters. I was surprised that I was the man here. That'd be called 'topping' if I was to use correct queer terminology but I didn't know that in 2002 so instead I thought, *I guess I'm the man here*. Then I grabbed her head and started kissing her.

We moved over to a bench and sat down, still getting off with each other. I touched one of her boobs through her top but the padding in her bra was rustling too much so I pulled it down. I couldn't work out if this was exciting 'cause I fancied girls or exciting 'cause I was so annoyed at the staff that I wanted to test the limits of what we couldn't do.

I'd had my hands down her pants for a minute when the door swung open. We flew apart. One of the Old Bitches poked her head round the door. 'Girls, leisure time is over.' The disbelief and relief that she didn't even realize was so huge that after a second of silence we blurted out the sweetest, most obliging innocent '*Okay*s' and smiles before heading back downstairs.

I had always felt very matter of fact about my bisexuality despite our Polish priest telling us to pray for the mentally ill homosexuals during the era of Section 28. I grew up confident about my queerness. Girls at school made fun of me for it but autism's lack of regard for social norms combined with my constant sapphic-novel-reading had given me confidence and I remained unruffled. I couldn't imagine being anything other than bisexual and never thought of it as weird. It took repeated messages, over and over and over again, to instil a suitable amount of shame in me.

From what I can tell, a lot of allistic people I know are primarily motivated by social approval so push any rogue queerness down into their subconscious or suppress their thoughts and only get comfortable with it later in life. For me, it's been the reverse. I was made to get uncomfortable with it. A combination of my rigid thinking with no grey areas combined with society's messages about sexuality made me more muddled than was necessary. My teen years would be the last time, for a long time, that I felt being bisexual was normal.

'Natalie said she came like 12 times.' Sadie nodded and smiled, puffing on her fag.

'Really?' I replied.

I wanted to feel proud but given I'd fingered her badly for under a minute this seemed unlikely, unless getting interrupted by septuagenarian healthcare assistants was her kink. I didn't say any of this though, reconciling myself to a reputation as the stud of the unit.

I don't recall anyone ever explaining to me what the dynamics or purpose of group therapy was. At Westleigh Way, there was little rhyme or reason to anything we did. They just plonked me in there one day and because I didn't know what I was meant to do I tended to say nothing and would watch it play out like a TV programme.

'Something exciting happened for Laura this week, didn't it?'

Laura's big kohl-rimmed eyes stayed fixed on the floor. You had to really concentrate to hear what she was saying as she spoke so softly it was barely audible.

'I went to see Marilyn Manson last night and it was fucking brilliant—'

I grinned in amazement. Hearing Laura speak to the group finally and let her enthusiasm override her crippling shyness was so cool. But before she could take any more shaky Bambi steps towards speaking, Lorraine swooped in with her catchphrase.

'Ah-ah-ah, that's not a Westleigh Way word now, Laura.'

Laura stammered and clammed up again, an oyster snapping shut.

Past the age of 12, as I broadened my reading, the more I studied English at school, the more I understood swearing with detachment and as simply another component of language. They'd taught us in English that swearing was what's called 'emotive language' – and once it had a designated function

I knew it wasn't what Catholics claimed it was, which was a sin so terrible you needed to tell the priest about it before reciting ten Hail Marys.

I'd started reading Irvine Welsh and knew from him that swearing could be used to illustrate anything from enthusiasm to emotion to dominance. It wasn't offensive, not really. Yet people's adherence to the social rules around swearing seemed a bit mad and appeared to focus disproportionately on women being protected from it at all costs. The mechanics in Dad's garage would swear then turn to me and apologize that I'd had to hear it. I'd wrinkle my nose, more offended at the apology than the curse.

If I understood all that as a kid, why couldn't the staff in the unit understand the need to let emotionally volatile people use emotive language when they needed to? Westleigh Way was all 'speak your truth – so long as it's comfortable and palatable to us'. In her study on how women are permitted to express anger and emotion, Soraya Chemaly notes that 'disapproval of swearing is based on social understandings of "male power and female purity." When women curse they tilt toward the "impure," and, in essence, are tacitly assumed to deserve punishment.'* This explained the attitude of Westleigh Way's staff, who seemed more concerned with chastising us for how we spoke than treating us as the patients we actually were.

I waited for Lorraine and the other staff to stop tutting and droning on about what everyone had been up to before tuning

---

* Chemaly, S (2018) *Rage Becomes Her: The Power of Women's Anger.* Atria Books.

back into the group. I caught the tail end of what Natalie was saying and her voice had gone trembly.

'. . . and that's why, ever since that fucking bastard raped me . . . I just cannae—'

'Natalie,' Lorraine said sharply, 'that's not how we speak here.'

I was stunned. Lorraine's admonishing her about the language policy while she was discussing the traumatic event that landed her there was something else. She tried to get Natalie to start again but – unsurprisingly – she'd clammed up. For the millionth time I wondered who exactly the unit was meant to serve.

They changed my timetable again to include more school and no therapy.

I heard from one of the girls that I'd been banned from group therapy as I was 'disruptive' and 'manipulative' – terms generally assigned to anyone in a support setting who doesn't monosyllabically agree with every aspect of their treatment.

Lorraine and I sat opposite each other in her office. There was a box of tissues on a side table between us.

'If I push these . . . here . . .' She moved the tissues a couple of inches to the right. 'Does that bother you?'

I looked at her in confusion. 'No.'

'What if I was to push them . . .' She made a sweeping motion moving them even further away. 'Over here?'

A smirk tugged at the muscles in my cheeks as I fought to suppress my laughter. 'No, that's fine.'

I was beginning to think Lorraine had a mental problem herself, batting tissues this way and that way around the table.

This was CBT, delivered very poorly in order to treat an obsessive-compulsive disorder I didn't have and that in no way applied to tissues. By this point, my faith in Lorraine was so low it seemed pointless explaining that I just needed everyone in my house to comply with putting my things in the right place and letting me stick to my routine. That had nothing to do with tidiness or thinking they'd die or that bad things would happen if they didn't do it. The bad thing that happened was that I would have to go and quietly cut myself in private because punching walls and headbutting things was unacceptable and not how nice girls behaved. That was the only session of one-to-one therapy I received the entire time I was there.

I'd been attending the unit for a few weeks with almost no improvement. I felt better from not being in a school environment, but my parents could have shut me in the garden shed with my schoolbooks and it would have had the same effect.

By now it was the Easter holidays and Mum had gone to work in Tesco while I sat watching TV with my brothers. I knew that I was due in the unit that day, even though everyone from normal school was off, but I hadn't got dressed yet. I didn't feel like it. The taunting from the staff, the silliness of therapy; it had stopped being fun or interesting. As I watched my brothers watching TV, it occurred to me that no one in the family ever acknowledged I was in the mental unit. Not at dinner, not in the morning, not when the taxi came to pick me up, not when I was dropped back home in the afternoons. If ever I was so bold as to mention it at dinner it was determinedly ignored, throats cleared, topics changed.

My mental breakdown was cloaked in silence even while it was happening in front of them.

'I'm not gonna go into the unit today,' I said out loud, testing the silence. My brothers barely turned round from the TV. 'You know, the mental unit I'm in?' I said, more to myself this time. Still nothing.

Since everyone else was pretending it didn't exist, I decided I could do that too. The taxi arrived and waited. The driver came to the door. I answered the door in my pyjamas and told him I wasn't going. I returned to the armchair in front of the TV and watched back-to-back episodes of *Heartbreak High* instead, resolutely ignoring the deafening silence from my brothers.

The next day, Lorraine and the Old Bitches were fuming. The response was way beyond what I had anticipated. I was kept behind after breakfast and called in to a meeting with them.

'You have lost your taxi privileges and will no longer be taking taxis to the unit.'

'Well how am I meant to get here?'

'You'll take the bus.'

'But I can't get a bus,' I said flatly. It was true. Mum tightly controlled things to such an extreme that I only knew how to get the bus to school and you didn't need money for that. You just walked to the bottom of the hill and got on.

'You *will* get a bus here,' they said firmly.

'I don't think you understand,' I said, slowly so they'd take it in. 'I don't know how to get a bus.'

They scoffed, no doubt thinking this was another attempt to manipulate them. I knew normally they were dealing with streetwise kids who bussed their way round West Lothian with impunity. I couldn't even catch a train to Edinburgh without getting overwhelmed and lost.

'You abused the taxi privilege.'

'I didn't! I—'

'You abused it and you have lost that privilege.' Again, being treated like I'd done something bad. I started to cry. Or didn't. I've realized since my diagnosis that there were a lot of times where I felt extreme distress but my face gave away absolutely nothing. I snapped my ankle a couple of years ago running for a train and couldn't stand up or move, the pain was so excruciating. When I rang the ambulance and then my boyfriend to send help, he told me later I sounded so calm he refused to believe anything was wrong with me. In fact, the more freaked out I felt, the more my voice flattened out to one tone.

Trying my hardest with staff, I made one last attempt to show them I was upset.

'I don't know how to get a bus, though.' My voice sounded strangled.

'You'll learn.'

It felt like everyone in our group was getting worse. *I* was getting worse, largely from the growing sense that I'd caused my family to keep a secret they didn't want. My mum had found the letter and necklace from Natalie and went ballistic, saying it was disgusting that I was stealing jewellery from a girl who was unwell. On top of that, my boyfriend had found out about Natalie and I and did not see me cheating on him with a girl as hot and porn-y. Meanwhile, Natalie had started talking dreamily about getting into Ward 17. 'One day . . .' She gazed into the middle distance. 'They'll put me there.'

'What's Ward 17?' I asked Sadie.

'That's where they put the adult psych cases. It's where I'll be soon.'

They had already reconciled themselves to being institutionalized for life. 'Reconciled' is the wrong word entirely, actually – they were excited for it. That was their career ladder. There were so few other appealing options for women in West Lothian that being a career psychiatric patient at least gave them a sense of purpose. I could already see the appeal – I had status in there, was more popular than I'd ever been in school and, even if I didn't have much in common with the others, they weren't like girls at school, who seemed to be continually plotting stuff behind your back, ready to make fun of your clothes, hair, voice or sexuality.

The more I learn about autism in women and how often we end up in CAMHS or other psychiatric units after imploding in high school (seriously, you can almost set your watch by it), the more I realize it's highly unlikely that I was the only autistic person in there. How many of them in Westleigh Way were undiagnosed? I'd wager Laura, with her lack of eye contact, her selective mutism, the fact that a relatively huge change had led her to shut down and go silent. If we'd actually been diagnosed with autism and received appropriate therapy (because allistic talking therapies are almost totally useless for autistics), none of us would have wasted our time in there. None of us would have built identities so early on that were rooted in the idea that we were bad, 'problem' girls somehow – identities that would follow us into our adult lives. The language policies that had been so carefully designed not to stigmatize us did nothing when we were consistently treated in such a way that we internalized the notion we were defective. CAMHS started a lot of us on a pathway that doomed us to be in and out of psychiatric treatment for pathologies we didn't have.

Even now, I struggle to see it as anything other than a grotesque waste of NHS money, time and resources.

I remember my sixteenth birthday clearly because I was in a mental unit having 'Happy Birthday' sung to me by the assembled patients and nurses. I managed to see my non-insane friends after, still a mishmash of goths and skater types. About six of us squeezed into my room and squished together on my bunkbed to eat Party Rings and listen to Smashing Pumpkins. Even though I'd been told I was depressed, I felt a pure happiness. I don't remember if anyone asked where I'd been, or if I ever told them, but I felt relieved I had quirky friends as it lessened my worry of what they'd think if they found out the truth.

I signed myself out of the unit shortly after my birthday. I scrawled on the big whiteboard 'FERN HAS LEFT THE BUILDING' and left to zero fanfare. There was no follow-up, no more psychiatrist appointments, no mention of further treatment from my parents. It was like it had never happened. Everyone acted like I was okay, so I figured that meant I was.

That August I got my exam results and got what I wanted. Three As and a B. Unconditional offers from every university I'd applied to.

I didn't have to kill myself for now.

Chapter Five

'One of the essential components of ASD is a difficulty
understanding the thoughts, feelings and intentions
of others – [for example] reading body language and if
you're not good at working out what someone's thinking
and feeling, how do you get that information? By reading
fiction. Because in the text is very clearly what someone
is thinking and feeling.'

—Tony Attwood, 'Autism in Females'[*]

I consistently made whoever I was going out with my special
interest.[†] I'm still hyper-aware of doing it now, mentioning my

---

[*] Attwood, T (2015) 'Autism in Females': www.youtube.com/watch?
v=wfOHnt4PMFo&t=417s
[†] The term 'special interest' refers to the autistic tendency to have intense
focused interests that bring us a lot of joy. We tend to bring them up at
every opportunity. The stereotypical idea of an autistic special interest

partner a little too much, a little too often, and have tried in vain to curb it to avoid derision. I only worked out that I was doing it when colleagues asked pointedly, 'How's your boyfriend?' and I worked my way backwards from there to understand it was a characteristically neurotypical way of saying that I mentioned him too much.

This is the kind of trait that gets missed in women, because playing the secondary character in your own life, orbiting around a man's wants and needs and his greatness, is so everyday – especially in working-class culture and especially where I'm from – that it never occurs to doctors when looking for special interests in autistic women that the intensity of their interest can manifest in *people*, not just things. The idea you can't be autistic because you've had a relationship is the biggest falsehood going in autistic women.

For many of us, our special interest *is* our romantic partner.

I had recently broken up with Adam.

I was distraught and stopped eating much. The feelings in my head and chest were so painful and overwhelming that the physical feeling of being hungry helped dull them.

I had a panic attack and, thinking I was dying, phoned the Samaritans and hyperventilated to them down the phone while I lay crumpled on the kitchen floor.

---

would be a boy who loves trains or *Star Trek*, but it can be anything. I feel uncomfortable every time I use the term, though, as it feels patronizing and pathologizes a harmless trait purely because allistics don't understand it. Such focuses are more likely to be described by autistic people as 'preoccupations' or 'passions', which are terms I prefer.

I was only a couple of months out of Westleigh Way and still decidedly bananas. My family had headed off on their annual summer holiday without me and I was trusted to be in the house alone for the first time. It would also turn out to be the last.

I was working on the reception at Dad's office for the summer. In between operating the switchboard and telling gruff haulage bosses to please hold for a moment, I phoned my ex's house repeatedly, pressing redial over and over and writing him love letters that I'd then stick in the laminating machine (laminating it meant more 'cause it's indestructible). I skipped lunch and chugged can after can of Diet Coke from the vending machine.

In the afternoon lull, I browsed the profiles on a gay dating site. Lauren and I had joined on our computers at school. I can't remember which one of us suggested that we should do it. Every weekend at her house we would watch a lesbian BBC period drama until we had watched all of them. But Lauren wasn't out; and while I knew I was bi, we were still doing everything under the guise of 'Aren't lesbians funny?' I don't think a lot of the Scottish LGBT community knew they were chatting to a pair of 16-year-olds. There were a fair few men catfishing as women but they were pretty easy to spot. There were also a lot of creepy couples looking for threeway partners. That's how I met Karen and Shaun.

A message pinged up from them while I was logged into the work computer. I slurped my tenth can of Diet Coke that day as I read it, clutching my side as I tapped out my reply one-handed. I had recently started to get a nagging pain there but had been ignoring it.

'We live in Glasgow. Can you drive through or do you want us to come get you?'

I explained that I couldn't drive, omitting the inconvenient fact that this was because I was a child. Karen and Shaun began messaging me every day regardless. They seemed pretty keen to do whatever they could to make things happen quickly.

While we were messaging, the pain in my side that had started in the office worsened considerably and brought with it a fever. An emergency doctor's visit revealed I had a kidney infection, likely brought on from my poor interoception* leading me to drink nothing but Diet Coke and reduce my food consumption down to one thing. Rather than ask anything about my diet or what might have caused my illness, the GP printed off a prescription for antibiotics and told me to rest for a week.

Meanwhile Karen and Shaun insisted it was no bother to pick me up that weekend and I agreed, grudgingly. It felt like I'd sort of passed the cut-off point where I could say no. I was still meant to be on bed rest when they came right up to our front door and knocked on it that Saturday. It was mad driving through Bathgate and all the way through to the suburbs of Glasgow with them, Karen chatting normally about her job as

---

* Interoception is the ability to notice and address internal bodily sensations. Poor interoception affects me even when I'm excited about stuff. (This is the case for lots of autistics.) I'll forget to drink or eat anything for hours or even move from the same spot as I become so absorbed in what I'm doing. When stressed or uncertain I reduce my foods down to two or three things and when very distressed my diet will become so unhealthy I end up with infections.

a policewoman, the two of them laughing as if we weren't all perverts who were going to hell.

When we got to their house, Karen cooked tortellini with tomato and mascarpone sauce, a dish that had only just landed in the supermarkets of suburban Scotland and was the height of sophistication. I sat on the couch sipping a Bacardi Breezer and looked at Karen's police uniform hanging over the door of the living room. It was a real uniform made of heavy fabric with a chain attached, not a sexy one from Anne Summers.

I ate the pasta sitting between the two of them on the couch and asked her about her job. She'd worked with prostitutes and seemed pro-decriminalization.

'Mostly I just feel sorry for them,' she said, handing me another alcopop.

She said this sadly, which was weird given she was about to have a threesome with a schoolgirl. I started thinking then how everyone said schoolgirls were sexy, how everyone in porn wanted to be us, but I didn't feel sexy at all. I just felt like an idiot. I couldn't see what was sexy about the fact I had transferred schools purely to study Advanced French after going mad.

As I sat between them on the couch, I had the overwhelming sense that I was trying to play a role without knowing any of the lines. On the other side of me Shaun started to rub my leg. Karen took all her clothes off and looking at her I remembered a pink inflatable pig I had seen on holiday once; it had been tethered above a pub and I think it had been advertising Danish bacon. I tried to remember what Andy Burns had told me at school about how to go down on a woman, something to do with spelling the alphabet out with your tongue. Karen suddenly seemed very old indeed. I didn't know how to say I didn't feel like it anymore, so I did it.

They had a big sports holdall in the centre of the room, which I'd failed to register earlier, filled with dildos and multipacks of batteries, many of which appeared to have been torn out of their packets and opened in haste. I wondered if this was how all childless couples lived, with holdalls of dildos lying around their living room instead of kids' toys. I thought how back at our house it was normal for us to have Virgin Mary ornaments and two types of holy water in our living room (one for special occasions, one for everyday use) so it seemed possible that their situation was more of a Protestant thing.

After the first round of sex, Karen cooked Spam for us and the sight of her naked while the fluorescent-pink meat sizzled in the pan made me feel bilious.

'Try it!' She thrust it towards me, the angry-looking meat sweating on the end of a fork.

'No thank you,' I said, barely able to hide my disgust. I had never met anyone who ate Spam before. It seemed likely it was the bad people Mum talked about, whose parents didn't love them and who ate Findus Crispy Pancakes and Dairylea Lunchables and let their teeth rot in their heads. I already knew Mum would hate me for this but the thought of her finding out I was eating processed food on top of everything else didn't bear thinking about.

They seemed to want to have sex endlessly whereas I felt like once had been more than enough. At one point I distracted Shaun from making a move by playing their piano and he in turn played a jazz number called 'Misty' with no clothes on. I offered to play my version of it even though my hands were too small to properly play jazz. Unfortunately, the naked piano-playing had made him even more amorous so, in a panic, I told them the latest episode of *Six Feet Under* was about to come on and I always watched it on Saturdays so would it be okay if I watched it please?

They petulantly agreed and the three of us sat in various states of undress on the sofa: me, delighted to have brought my soothing Saturday routine into this alarmingly unfamiliar situation; them pretending to watch, all the while impatiently glancing over at the holdall of dildos.

My kidneys were really hurting but I felt like kidney pain wasn't on the list of appropriate conversation topics at a threeway.

As the credits ended, I could feel they were both impatient to have more horrible sex. I knew I couldn't ask for a lift home as both of them had been drinking since we got back there and it was way too far to get a taxi with the zero pounds I had in my purse. After much pestering from Shaun to come upstairs I fell asleep on the couch, insisting I'd head up once I'd finished watching a David Attenborough documentary. When I woke up, Shaun had come downstairs and wanted to have sex again so I grudgingly obliged. Then he took me upstairs where the three of us all had to lie in their bed together doing sexy laughing. I lay there stiffly. I hated sexy laughing more than anything. My eyes glanced around the room, trying to make out objects in the semi-darkness to get my bearings. Karen saw me glancing at a huge candle on a chest of drawers and they both started giggling about how she'd shoved it up her fanny once.

Right then and there I upped the ante on asking them to

drive me home. They seemed hurt that I didn't want to keep going and live this debauched Bacchanalian hell-life. I guess as working adults they had to wring every last bit of enjoyment out of their weekends whereas it was my summer holidays – I had acres of time. Karen was on the clock and would have to be back on the beat come Monday, arresting prostitutes and solving crimes.

'Can I go home please? I'm a bit tired,' I asked again in the gloom, trying to avoid touching them. I felt really sick now. When they were slow to get up I got up and got dressed, going downstairs.

I was back in their living room, fully clothed at last and pacing back and forth agitatedly. The two of them were really making a meal out of putting their shoes on and finding the car keys as slowly as possible so I looked through their DVDs to avoid talking to them.

'Are you sure you want to go? We thought you'd stay all weekend?' Karen sounded disappointed.

'Yeah, no, sorry . . . I have to get back,' I replied. I pulled out one DVD and examined it.

'Well, maybe you can come back next weekend?' she said. I looked over my shoulder and saw Shaun and her exchanging hopeful glances.

I turned back to the DVD rack so they couldn't see my eyes widen. Who the *fuck* did this every weekend?

'Yeah! Yeah, that'd be great,' I lied. No way was I coming back next weekend. I wasn't going to work as their sex slave. They were lucky they'd got me for one night. I wasn't sure what I hated more, the sex or all the giggling sexy small talk in between. I didn't really think it right to laugh, the jollity felt incongruous with what was basically Satanic.

'You can borrow that DVD if you like. Just bring it back when we next see you,' Shaun grinned.

I smiled tightly and slipped it in my bag.

'Just one more thing. We *have* to show you this before you go. Shaun, go get them from the cupboard.'

Oh no. I was all sexed-out. I watched as Shaun rummaged around in a cupboard, wondering if he was going to show me Polaroids of the time they stretched Karen's bumhole out by stuffing kitchen utensils up there.

He pulled out two enormous stuffed animals and with some trepidation placed them at opposite corners of the room. They were the size of toddlers. Karen was more excited than when I'd been going down on her.

'Switch them on!' she squealed, clapping delightedly.

Shaun fidgeted with them, pressing some switch on at the back. The animals, Looney Tunes characters, a rabbit and a duck, stiffly started to speak to each other across the room with pre-programmed phrases, their big glass eyes betraying their terror. Karen and Shaun both laughed, looking at me expectantly as if I was going to be blown away by this feat of modern technology.

'Oh right . . . that's great,' I said with zero conviction.

'Aren't they brilliant?' They both grinned at me maniacally.

Given that autistic people are the ones meant to be unable to read non-verbal cues, it still astonishes me that when my face and voice are telling people I have no interest in something, they try to force a response I don't have. I started to worry that if I didn't lie and say yes, Karen and Shaun would keep me there forever.

'Yeah,' I said, trying harder to sound more engaged but it came out flat.

Looking crestfallen, Karen picked up the car keys.

On the drive home they were laughing and chatting while I sat mute in the back. They could almost have been my friends' parents driving me home from a sleepover. I slumped down in the back seat hoping no one I knew would catch sight of me in their car as we arrived back in Bathgate. I badly wanted to shut the car door behind me, put as much distance as I could between me and them and pretend like this had never happened.

It took me years to realize that, no matter how grown-up you think you are, adults can tell when you're a kid.*

The night after, Lauren came over to stay at my still-empty house and I decided to tell her the whole thing. We laughed about it and it felt good having a story that made her laugh as I wasn't much use when we were in a large group at school. I decided I liked having these unusual experiences and that it probably made me quite urbane. Like a woman in a novel.

---

* Later, I did material on this experience in a stand-up routine but couldn't say, 'I was a schoolkid,' as it wouldn't have been relatable or funny then. It's barely relatable as it is. The material then got made into a light-hearted sketch for some stupid TV show and seeing the whole thing reduced down to cartoonish silliness gave me a feeling I couldn't explain.

A few days later, Rosie and Jim, an elderly couple who lived across from my parents' house and had a clear view into our living room, told my mum about a strange man and woman who'd been to our front door to pick me up. When my mum questioned me I told her that they were my friend's parents. This was unconvincing as Shaun was black and everyone we knew was exceptionally, uniformly white. Mum raised an eyebrow at my explanation but said nothing more.

Things degenerated to such an extent that Mum kicked me out repeatedly. This would have been less of an issue if I hadn't been so mollycoddled in the preceding years that I struggled to even catch a bus on my own. The first time she kicked me out I cried in a panic and packed my essentials (*The Journals of Sylvia Plath*, Anne Sexton's *The Awful Rowing Toward God*, another book about Sylvia Plath and Ted Hughes's breakup). The Plath diaries took up most of the space in my schoolbag so, trying to think of more essentials, I stuffed one pair of pants down the side along with my Prozac, some mascara and eyeliner. I decided my toothbrush, deodorant or clean clothes would have to wait. I used the last of my money to get a bus to Linlithgow, where my new school was, and messaged two goth girls who were the closest thing I had to friends there. They met me off the bus and I cry-walked through the street, the goths seemingly relieved to finally have some darkness in their too-pleasant lives. I walked into a corner shop with my new friends, who were patting and reassuring me as I heaved, 'But I don't know what I'm going to do-o-o!'

'What's going on here?' Mo, the notoriously grumpy owner of the shop, softened when he saw me.

'She's been kicked out,' they replied in unison.

I filled my days by visiting the local library alone, checking my Gaydar Girls account to connect with my true friends, the lesbians of the internet. I replied to a student in Edinburgh who talked to me about Jeanette Winterson books and her Ph.D thesis.

Seeing another notification, I grimaced. Karen and Shaun had messaged to say they wanted their *Human Traffic* DVD back. Well, they could piss off; I had bigger things to worry about.

I found myself left with no option but to sofa surf on various schoolfriends' pull-out mattresses, but most people's parents didn't want to get involved and very quickly I was down to one friend whose mum was divorced and read the *Guardian* and didn't mind taking me in. The uncertainty of the whole thing was so unbearable that I couldn't concentrate on anything else and existed purely on a day-to-day basis, thinking only about my next meal and how to fill my days.

As I'd already been accepted to university a year early, I figured it made sense to stop going to school completely and instead continued to go to the library, where I checked out multiple books and read more than ever. I also visited Mo in his shop as he'd offered to help me out with my Arabic before I went off to university. I'd sit on a little stool beside him behind the counter and read the newspapers while he served customers.

'What star sign are you?' I asked him.

He furrowed his brow. 'Hmm. I am Leo.'

I started reading his horoscope out loud. He spotted

something out the window of the shop and stiffened but I kept reading.

'With Capricorn in your house of love you'll find that—'

He froze, looking outside as he held up a finger to silence me. 'Listen – shh, shh – my wife is coming in the shop. You tell her you are working for me as a shop assistant.'

'Oh, okay.'

She came in and they chatted tersely in Urdu for a bit while I carefully rehearsed the line in my head: 'I am working as an assistant in the shop. I am working as an assistant in the shop . . .' All the while wondering why he'd asked me to say that.

Even though I never asked, Mo assured me afterwards that they were getting a divorce; it was just taking his wife a while to accept it. I nodded and tried to look understanding but had no idea what any of this meant. He tried to cheer me up by taking me to the Pizza Hut all-you-can-eat buffet at the local shopping centre.

'Why aren't you eating anything?' I asked through a mouthful of deep-pan.

He shook his head and just watched me eat, his brow furrowed and mouth turned down at the corners, a Basset Hound of a man. I wondered why people were staring at us. It didn't occur to me that a white schoolgirl eating with an elderly Pakistani man was an odd sight in West Lothian.

'You should go home.'

I sighed, rolling my eyes. 'I told you I can't go home. Every time I go home, Mum kicks me out again. Can you tell me more about the Quran?'

There was a silence between us.

'They don't want me to come home. My mum hates me.'

Mo said nothing, still staring at me. I pulled the stuffed crust off my pizza and started to tear it into little pieces, arranging them into a pattern on the plate.

'My dad wants me to come home, I think. He texted me asking where I am.'

'I will take you home.'

In the car outside my house, he topped up my phone for me. *Maybe this is* zakat, *the Muslim form of charity*, I thought to myself. *What a kind man.*

'Any time you need help you call me.'

'Will you be okay, Mo?'

He stared ahead, looking miserable. 'You need to go home.'

'Okay,' I said, getting out the car reluctantly.

'Bye.'

I never knew what to make of Mo until I saw a TV show about the grooming scandals of vulnerable girls in the North of England and was staggered that the initial grooming process matched my experience entirely. Autistic girls are way more vulnerable to grooming and exploitation. Combine the fact we make friends with anyone who is kind to us with our tendency to experience social exclusion within our peer group and it's unlikely anyone is going to be around to tell you that actually, that 60-year-old man might not have your best interests at heart.

School didn't teach me about stuff like this and my parents certainly didn't either, so I had to use books as my guide. But even they didn't cover everything.

*

I'd not been back at the house long when my dad came to pick me up from my shift at Tesco one Sunday evening. I didn't realize he wasn't really speaking until he started to drive, not in the direction of our house less than a mile away but speeding towards the motorway.

'Where are we going?'

'We're going to the police station.'

'Huh?'

'They're arresting you for smoking marijuana.'

I screwed up my face in utter confusion. 'But I haven't smoked it? Dad! Turn the car around!'

He revved up and drove faster. 'Yes you have. Stop lying!'

Aghast at the injustice and frantically trying to untangle where he'd got this from, I blurted out: 'I haven't! I dunno what you're even talking about! If anyone should be getting arrested it's Sean – he's the one smoking it on the bus to school every day!'

Still speeding along, I spotted a flicker of doubt in Dad's eyes as he looked sidelong at me, trying to compute the possibility that the angelic baby of the house could do anything wrong. Wordlessly, he turned the car around at the next roundabout and sped back to our house.

What followed is still one of the dumbest things my parents have done. They spent a torturously long evening doing a bad cop/bad cop interrogation of my brother and I, convinced we were drug addicts and keeping it a secret from them.

'If you don't admit it now, you're getting arrested,' Mum shrieked in her terrible banshee wail while Dad paced in the background.

I'd given up making logical sense of their behaviour by this stage so I mentally retreated as far as possible inside my head, attempting to watch the scenario from a distance as if it was some bizarre TV show that had nothing to do with me.

Mum stepped back, clinging on to the fireplace and shouting that she may as well drive off a bridge and kill herself. This was the cue for Dad to step forward to give us his final warning.

'I knew a laddie who smoked marijuana. Thought he was being clever. He was found *dead* behind the back of West Lothian College!'

I burst out laughing. Unless the guy OD'd on Kettle Chips and Oreos it sounded highly unlikely.

After I'd repeated upwards of 20 times that I hadn't smoked weed, my parents finally admitted that the police arrest was made up as a ruse between them so they could force us to admit 'the truth'. This was so insane I vowed at this point to cut them out of my life as soon as I left home.

Leaving the house later, I saw the opaque figure of my younger brother through the glass door and heard him pleading, 'Dad, Dad, please: I'll do anything not to be like her.'

I asked Dad years later about this scene and he explained I'd been acting oddly – so naturally, setting up a fake police interrogation to finagle a confession out of me was the best way to address this. They'd looked at my withdrawn state and grown suspicious. It was likely I was doing some or all of the following:

Sleeping a lot as soon as I got home from school, often fully-clothed

Staying in my bedroom to stim by rocking in my
    rocking chair
Not speaking much
Acting spaced out

And together they'd concluded I was stoned.

My parents' overprotectiveness was undermined by a marked naivety that meant they often looked for answers to problems in all the wrong places.

What might have worked better was looking at how much change there was in my life: changing school, changing job, their unsettling habit of kicking me out the house every week – something I imagine would be challenging for any teen never mind an autistic one. My routine – one of the only calming and regulating forces in an autistic's life – was upended on a daily basis. All I needed was a quiet place to recharge from masking my autistic traits, which I was having to do non-stop at my new school as well as at my new job at Tesco. Autistics do not deal with change well. Switching school was a disastrous idea for me because a change like that for an autistic is as big as having a child or moving country for most people. We are at our most low-functioning when we experience big changes and lose some or all of our ability to mask. With no other information or answers to hand, this was instead read by my parents as bad behaviour.

After the theatrics of that night and with my time at Westleigh Way still fresh in my memory, I realized that trying to be well-behaved did nothing to stop my parents' determination to cast me as the black sheep of the family. So I decided to do everything they'd accused me of doing.

I started smoking weed. A girl on the Tesco checkouts used old till receipts to draw me a diagram demonstrating how to roll the perfect joint. I brought one of the nightshift guys back to have sex in the house when my parents were out. After they found out about both these things I had a physical fight with Mum and she kicked me out again. When she came in for her own Tesco shift (at this point everyone we knew worked in Tesco so it truly had replaced the village square or church as a central hub of the community), she blanked me as I sat at the checkout. I had to beg her to bring my work shoes in. She handed them over without looking at me.

I started hanging about with my older cousin's friends, who were all in their mid-twenties and *real* adults. I was 17. I hooked up with one, Calum, then started dating another, a chubby doe-eyed stoner called Fat Scott. I felt indifferent to Scott but he liked the same music as me, always had weed and, crucially, had a car that could take me out of Bathgate. (As an adult in a script-development meeting years later, I tried to explain in vain to a hipster TV producer that yes, girls in small shitty towns date guys with cars purely so they can get lifts to places. He told me this was unrealistic and Not A Thing.)

Scott wrote a short story about me and to my toe-curling horror read it out in the car. The story was filled with admiring talk of my mystery and enigma and coolness and, bafflingly, included the description 'she moves with a sexy arrogance'. I don't move with a sexy arrogance. I've seen myself on camera. Like most autistics, I have coordination and gait problems that lead to me kicking drinks across the carpet every day and tripping over my own feet while out walking. Never underestimate the willingness of men to project their own feminine ideals onto women, where autism in a cute girl can be misread as Mysterious, as Aloof, as Arrogant.

Lauren exploded with laughter reading Scott's story one night.

'What's he on about? You crash into stuff all the time! And all this stuff about how enigmatic you are? I bet you just had cats dancing to music in your head the whole time.'

We wiped away tears as we took turns reading it out, stopping to laugh at every other sentence. It was a relief to have at least one friend who had an accurate understanding of me. Outside of that, I had no idea who I was.

In my parents' house I was told I was evil and clever. In school I was strange and quiet.

To people trying to have sex with me I was mysterious and sexy.

None of these things fitted, but Lauren had seemed to perceive immediately that I had no clue what was going on in social situations and accepted it without question.

Dad eventually let me go back to the house. During another argument I told my parents that I'd told the school they'd kicked me out and that the headmaster might make a referral to social services. My dad spluttered, genuinely incredulous, his voice going up in pitch.

'You – you cunt!'

I'd never heard him say the word before. I was so stunned that I didn't register his hand swooping through the air and hitting me until I landed on the ground. I picked myself up, headed to my room and numbly gathered my things, packing

Sylvia Plath and Anne Sexton yet again, the same stupid ritual. I went to my magazine rack, pulling out tightly packed copies of *Cosmo* and the *NME* and digging for the money I was sure I'd hidden between the pages. There was none left. I realized I had nothing and no credit on my phone. I left and walked fast down the hill, crying. I went to the phone box and used my last pound in the world to call Lauren.

'Can you come get me from the bottom of the hill?'

'Oh my god, are you okay?'

'Quick, I'm on a payphone. Just come meet me.'

She whizzed to our town in her car and sat listening to me wailing. Her car, the fact she was a year older than me and her sense of calm concern made her feel almost maternal.

'You can't come stay at mine but here's money for a train to Edinburgh.'

I took the train, my thoughts racing, trying to work out what I was supposed to do from there. No one had prepared me for this. My parents' overprotectiveness seemed like a joke given they'd now turfed me out with zero coping skills. I got to Edinburgh and walked through the Meadows trying to find Fat Scott's flat in pitch-darkness. I have no sense of direction and smartphones hadn't been invented yet so I'd memorized his directions in my head, saying them over and over to myself as I walked.

It was nightmarish and I got lost repeatedly. I thought back to the stories I'd heard of girls getting raped there in the dark and the whole pitch-black expanse seemed to spin around me. I started walking this way and that and through my panic realized that I was walking in useless circles. Eventually

Fat Scott rang my mobile, surprised at the state I was in, and directed me to his flat.

He wore a synthetic football top in bed. The feel and sound of it rustling over his lardy belly made me want to puke. He tried to hug me and I stiffened as my skin screamed at the shiny fabric scratching against it.

'Please take that off, it's disgusting.'

He laughed and smiled, taking it off. *Naw, on second thoughts, mate – put it back on.* I tried to hide a grimace. His subservience to me was repellent. I resigned myself to having to live with this man for the summer until I got into university accommodation in September. On balance it wasn't the worst – he always had drugs, gave me money to play the quiz machine in the pub and when he was out at work in the day I could read books in peace with no one bothering me; but my intense dislike of his face, body and smell meant I was fairly cold to him on a regular basis.

One night we went to Calum's flat to have drinks. All through school I was pretty sure that all I needed to not feel left out was to be around real adults. After all, no one at school had the same interests as me, probably 'cause I was so grown-up that I needed to be around adults. Except, when I hung around Karen and Shaun or Mo or my older boyfriend and his friends it was just a new kind of loneliness, but one where I thought hopefully, *Maybe when I'm their age I'll fit in.*

When we arrived there were probably four of us there, the others smoking weed and drinking, talking about their adult jobs and me occasionally trying and failing to think of a cool thing to say about books. Things were pleasant enough until Calum's new girlfriend showed up. She'd been drinking on a work's night out before coming back and it was evident from the off that she was jealous or insecure of the fact that I'd fucked Calum before she did. She walked into the living room, saying hi to all the guys in turn before regarding me coldly. She plonked herself down on an armchair opposite me and started a relentless stream of passive-aggressive comments in the guise of normal conversation. She made terse small talk with my boyfriend, smiling tightly. 'Good job? How's the new flat?' She thought she knew his flatmate.

Then she added: 'You'd be a nice guy if you weren't going out with a wee lassie.'

He laughed nervously. People around him attempted to change the topic, move onto something else, but her dozy, pished eyes were fixed on me.

'Stupid wee lassie,' she muttered as she stood up and put Mercury Rev on the CD player. She started to croon along tunelessly.

'And now the dark is rising! And a brand-new moon is born!'

She shook her head, inhaling her fag and muttering to herself before singing again.

'I dinnae get it, though. What you doing with her, man? Stupid wee lassie like that.'

I started to feel my breath quicken. A terrible adrenaline rush lit up my nervous system again and I felt dizzy as my heart pounded through my chest. Curled up in an armchair, Sian was still burbling away, her eyes closed as she sang.

'I never dreamed I'd lose you! In my dreams I'm always strong . . .'

In an instant, I stood up and walked over to the table and

picked up a bottle of vodka, my back to her. My plan was to tip it over her. I turned around and walked over.

'I'm not a wee lassie. I'm actually about to start uni,' I said, trying to seem assertive; but my voice was shaking and I sounded terrified. How many more women would get to just say stuff about me while I meekly sat there and took it? There were the women in Tesco, Lorraine in the mental unit, the girls at school, the teachers, Mum.

Why did I never do anything about it? It was pathetic, embarrassing. I felt repulsed at how weak I was.

I reached where she was sitting and silently tipped the full litre of vodka over her head. She squealed and as I watched it soak her as if in slow motion, something in me snapped. I flipped the full ashtray in her lap over her and before I knew it, I was hitting her over the head with the bottle. The song was a big sweeping orchestral number and the violins swelled as she screamed. It was a preposterous song to bottle someone to.

As I made contact with her skull everyone in the room leaped from their chairs in a collective 'Woah-woah-woah!' moment. In the commotion that followed, someone pulled me off her and before I knew it I was being dragged out the house. Someone – possibly me – was telling Scott to drive. Calum ran out the house screaming abuse at me and ripping his shirt open, which I felt was unnecessarily dramatic. He pounded the windows as Scott frantically tried to start the car, going, 'Oh fuck, oh god, oh fuck . . .' When we drove off, Scott asked over and over, 'Why did you do that? Why did you do that?' while I stared straight ahead in disbelief.

Later I found out that Sian had needed some butterfly

stitches. I was amazed slash horrified I'd caused an injury. Meek little me. Stupid wee lassie. The bottle had felt like nothing in my hand. Making contact had felt like nothing. I hadn't seen what other choice I had. The way I saw it at the time, if I hadn't have done that she would have attacked me first.

Having said that, Sian wasn't wrong: it *was* odd that a man was dating a teenager eight years younger than him. The way she made her point wasn't great but the adult me thinks it's a fair one. I understand now that a lot of people use alcohol to say what they're too scared to say normally and that as one of the only sober people in the room I was actually in a position of power. Had I known that, I could have either sat calmly while she needled me then taken her down verbally or said nothing and found a way to leave the party. I've been in similar situations dozens of times since and been unfazed and it makes me realize how utterly terrified I was at 18. Terrified of everyone and constantly hypervigilant.

Through years of practise, I can think a little more laterally now and am able to separate my autistic instincts from my actual behaviour by forcing myself to look at a situation from several angles. Initially, this wasn't easy but I now have an ability to think objectively that I didn't have before. I understand that my body overreacts due to my amygdala being too large and so I must mentally talk down a disproportionate fight-or-flight response that perceives any loud noises, shouting, confusing facial expressions or tones of voice as immediate threats.

Research has shown that the amygdala is either enlarged or too small in autistic people, which explains why we perceive aggression and certain emotions so differently from others. In autistic girls with depression and anxiety it tends towards the large side.* We cannot ignore the fact that nurture interacts with nature in these kinds of responses. As social animals, human beings have good reasons to feel physically unsafe when we are ostracized socially,† plus autistic people often bank up a lot of the trauma that we experience through life‡ and that inevitably affects how we perceive or act on certain emotions.

I now use data to reassure myself that if someone starts making bitchy comments at a party, no matter how frightening or uncomfortable it feels, it's statistically extremely unlikely that any violence will occur because the vast majority of people have a strong desire to avoid negative social consequences and avoid losing stuff like their freedom, money or status. I've learned all this from reading and studying humans like a Martian. *None* of it is intuitive.

I had absolutely no insight into this incident for a decade and nor did I have any understanding of why it happened. Instead, I learned from careful observation of others that I absolutely

---

* Schenkman, L (2020) 'Enlarged amygdala linked to severe behavioral problems in autistic girls'. *Spectrum News.* www.spectrumnews.org/news/enlarged-amygdala-linked-to-severe-behavioral-problems-in-autistic-girls/

† Some research into the long-lasting pain of ostracism can be found here: www.purdue.edu/newsroom/research/2011/110510Williams Ostracism.html

‡ One example of research that is being done to explore the links between autism and trauma and how this may manifest itself in PTSD can be found here: www.spectrumnews.org/features/deep-dive/intersection-autism-trauma/

should not tell people that she made me hit her and I had no option but to do it.

I used to shrug when people asked about it. I'd say, 'It was a difficult time. I was homeless and she would have hit me first.' Yet my inability to see shades of grey meant I had very little capacity to comprehend that there were other options.

It was only on my first day working in a halfway house for ex-offenders, almost a decade later, that it all clicked into place. My manager, an ex-offender himself, said simply: 'Here are everyone's case files. Sit down and read. Then let us know if you can do the job.'

Hunched over my desk reading one messy life story after another, I realized that almost everyone who kills someone isn't deranged or a maniac – they put those people in a different place, in the secure units, and their release is tightly managed by specialists. The offenders I worked with were more often than not intensely vulnerable, impulsive people with chaotic lifestyles who had made a terrible split-second error of judgement that permanently changed the course of their lives. The same sort of case came up again and again: people who had had a drunken argument and hit their partner or relative over the head – often with a bottle – and the person died later of a subdural haematoma. No one meant to do it.

My stomach lurched reading their case studies as I realized if I'd hit Sian an inch to the right or left, if I'd hit her harder or if I'd hit her twice, I'd be in prison for manslaughter. I may even have been diagnosed in there. Many autistic people don't get diagnosed until they're in prison. In addition to her diagnostic work, my therapist works within the criminal-justice sector and says one of the biggest problems for autistic clients when they go to appeal their sentences is their unabashed honesty. Most people will understand the unspoken implication that to win an appeal they have to parrot out a convincing apology and display remorse. I don't operate that way, at least not intuitively. I'd never say I regretted something unless I actually did.

Around the time of working in the halfway house I wrote a newspaper article about this incident, giving my insight into and understanding of why on earth I hit a relative stranger when I had no previous criminal history. I was still so lacking in self-awareness I can barely recall it now without cringing. I tried to explain the experience as 'going through a phase of behaving like Begbie in *Trainspotting*'. This is absolute nonsense. The character of Begbie has a thirst for violence and is well versed in it, dealing in it like a currency. Perhaps I thought it made me sound cool and hard and scary and streetwise; plus it played into well-established British media tropes around Scottish people and aggression. I couldn't exactly say in a national newspaper that I felt small and scared for my life.

Again, though, I was continually over-identifying with fiction to try and find a template for myself and my story – and there was no fiction available to describe being a girl who thinks the world is out to get her and after years of taunts finally lashes out.

Chapter Six

'you fit into me
like a hook into an eye

a fish hook
an open eye'

—Margaret Atwood, 'You Fit Into Me'

Mum was already stationed in the car outside and wailing as Dad left the student accommodation in Edinburgh's Old Town. This felt more than a little ridiculous given the fact I hadn't been living with them and had only gone back that morning from Fat Scott's place to pick up the last of my stuff. I watched them leave from the window, feeling nothing. Scrap that – as the car disappeared round the corner I felt euphoric. My own room! I didn't have to live with my loud family or some chunker in an acrylic tracksuit. I promised myself that from this point onwards, I would do whatever it took to never go back to Bathgate. To go back was unthinkable.

Two girls from Shetland that I met in halls took me out drinking in freshers' week. As we stood in the queue to an eighties-themed roller disco at the student union, the Shetland girls talked in hoarse voices with endless rolling *rrrrrr*s. One of them was insisting it was definitely legal for women to piss outside.

From behind us a posh English voice said loud enough for us to hear: 'Ugh! What's that smell?'

On cue, another voice replied: 'Smells like commoners!'

Pahahahaha.

Peals of horsey laughter ensued. I turned round to look. Two girls with artfully messy blonde hair wearing pearl necklaces were smirking back at me. That was the moment I realized that university wasn't going to be some idyll where everyone who was a geek at school bonded over books and the life of the mind.

Inside the student union, some 6-foot blond guy approached me. I'd not seen many men this height, proper big, unfeasibly healthy-looking adult men. Everyone at home was wizened and tiny from generational poverty. He said nothing to me but grabbed me, lifted me up and started kissing me, slamming me up against a wall. *This is the life!* I thought. This was how I'd seen freshers' week depicted on telly and in books and I was *here for it*.

At some point I peeled myself off him to go to the toilet. As I dried my hands and checked how far my mascara had run down my face, I noticed some girl scowling at me in the mirror before she pointedly told the Shetland girls how disgusting I was. I still don't understand this mad way of fighting – where women can only ever start a fight by using other women to communicate their message, like ghosts through a medium. I turned to address the little jury of girls in earnest, trying to appeal to their better judgement.

'But have you *seen* him? He's fit!'

I felt like the evidence I'd presented to the court in response to the question, 'Why are you getting off with that guy?' was clearly compelling; it was more than adequate from my point of view. Unfortunately, 'Because he's fit' and 'Because I wanted to' did not fly in 2004. They glared at me again as I walked out, muttering under their breath about how strange I was.

It was getting tiring, this. Girls seemed angry when you had sex unless you pretended you were in love. It felt like if you did what you wanted, if you had any agency, they felt you were taking something away from them – and that didn't make sense at all. I wasn't sure what exactly I had taken away from them by doing what I wanted. I guess if I enjoyed sex and didn't feel there were any consequences, I was robbing them of the idea that chastity was vital for social approval and a way of being held in high esteem. It was tribal.

I lived in a flatshare of five girls randomly put together by the university. One of the Shetland girls, Callie, had a go at me for bringing too many guys back to the flat that week. Callie was only in Edinburgh to do her law degree before returning home to Shetland to get married. She had packs and packs of bacon in the fridge, multipacks of smoky-bacon crisps and this weird hunk of dried salted meat that she shrieked with delight at when it arrived in thick bubblewrap from Shetland.

'Ma reestit mutton is here! Och, I love my reestit mutton!' They really were more Vikings than Scottish.

She opened the *Shetland Times* eagerly. 'Farmer Loses Sheep' was the front-page headline, with the sub-heading 'Found later that afternoon'.

'Oh look: ma ex-boyfriend's been electronically tagged.'

She popped some more dried-sheep jerky in her mouth before looking at me grimly.

'You're disgustin', you know.'

'Why?'

'Well, don't you think it's a bit much?'

I furrowed my brow in confusion. 'Well . . . No, because there's seven days in the week and I only brought back four guys.'

We all went on a flatmates' day trip to the STD clinic. I had no STDs whatsoever. One of the other girls had chlamydia from her so-called loving relationships. I was secretly smug all the way home, knowing the connection between virtue and virus was a scam.

I didn't know what I was supposed to eat now that I was living independently so I decided to only eat bagels as they were simple and didn't overwhelm me plus I liked their shape. Trying to work out what was a normal meal was too much when I had absolutely no idea how to find out where my classes were, how to electronically submit essays – basically how to do anything that everyone else seemed able to do effortlessly. If you're allistic you likely take for granted that when you're not sure of something you'll ask someone for help. Autism is so insular and self-contained that for us, asking for help sometimes feels like going against our nature. The dropout rate for autistic students is ten times higher than for non-autistic students and it's thought that's because most students tend to help each other by 'crowdsourcing' information from their peers.[*]

I found speaking to anyone on my course hard enough and my Arabic tutor had already taken the piss out of my accent so it didn't even occur to me to ask others how to do anything. I was two weeks in when I summoned up the guts to give it a go with a girl on my course.

'Hey, do you know where they put the reading list for this class?'

She grimaced at me. 'You shouldn't need to be *spoon-fed* here.'

It felt weird to be told this by someone who had likely had hundreds of thousands of pounds thrown at her education to get a place on the same course I'd got onto for free. Still, I was so ashamed about needing more help than others that I made sure not to ask anyone a single question for the rest of my time there.

My student grant was based on what my parents earned so I got an insane £80 a month to live on and pay my rent for the entire academic year. For context, I would have got two or three times that amount on unemployment benefit. Confusingly, my

---

[*]   Gurbuz, E et al (2019) 'University Students with Autism: The Social and Academic Experiences of University in the UK'. *Journal of Autism and Development Disorders*. link.springer.com/content/pdf/10.1007/s10803-018-3741-4.pdf

parents were insisting to me that they were skint. Given my rent was £400 a month, I ran out of money almost immediately and told them I didn't have enough money to live on. They promised to sort it and to come through for a visit to help me out. I was amazed at how supportive they were being and wondered if they'd be like Callie's dad, who let her order whatever she wanted from Tesco on his card. I waited for Dad all day, relieved that him and Mum had relented and finally understood that I'd need a lot more help for the rest of the academic year.

Dad arrived with an air of benevolence and handed me a frozen lasagne and a pair of new pyjamas. I stared at the lasagne in mute disbelief. It was so absurdly inadequate that I wondered whether it was a joke. I wanted to throw it back in his face. I couldn't pay my rent in lasagnes. I couldn't buy textbooks with lasagnes. I couldn't buy more food with lasagnes. I explained that I also didn't have a laptop and you needed one of those for university to do all your coursework. Dad promised to sort it and a week later brought some ancient IBM number from the 1980s he'd found at his work. It had no word-processing software on it nor indeed anything at all that would enable me to use it for writing or submitting essays. It still had dirt in its keyboard from the truckers at his garage. It took a while for me to realize how truly fucked I was and because neither of them went to university, I didn't know how to explain to them in a nice way that none of this was useful. When I looked up from angrily tapping keys on the laptop's blank screen, Dad was smiling at me hopefully.

'I know it's old but that'll be enough for your essays, eh?' I didn't want to seem ungrateful for my antique unusable computer so I nodded. Every time I opened the fridge and saw the lasagne I felt furious.

Dad was less cheery the next time I heard from him.

'The police turned up at the house looking for you. You need to go to Bathgate police station. They're going to arrest you.'

Fuuuuuuuuuuuuuuuuuck!

I had forgotten about Fat Scott. My boxes in student accommodation were barely unpacked before I'd dumped him unceremoniously by refusing to answer the door when he came to visit. I'd got my flatmate to hand him a box filled with all his stuff. A more Machiavellian person would have had the foresight to understand that the second I did this he was going to give his mates permission to go straight to the police. Evidently, I didn't have the theory of mind* to understand other folks' mental processes; I just wanted to get as far away from the guy as possible.

On hearing about my upcoming arrest, my housemates took me to the pub to try and calm me down. They patted my back while I flipped out, struggling to get enough air. If I couldn't handle school, I definitely wouldn't be able to handle prison.

---

* Theory of mind is the ability to understand other people's intentions, thoughts and beliefs. It's long been the assumption that autistic people have impaired theory of mind when in actual fact autistic people suffer from a double empathy problem – while we may struggle to interpret allistic behaviour we at least make an effort to understand it, an effort that isn't often reciprocated by allistic people. It's also been found we generally understand our fellow autistic people just fine.

'Only wear mascara, no eyeliner on the bottom rim. You want your eyes to look as round as possible.'

I nodded along as they planned an innocent eye-makeup look for my date with the police.

I wondered out loud whether I'd have to barter sexual favours off women in prison in exchange for food or tampons.

At the station I asked solemnly: 'Am I going to go to prison?'

The policeman scoffed gently at this. I didn't understand why he was laughing. You do a bad thing, you break the rules – you go to prison, surely?

'No, no, no. They won't send a wee girl like you.'

I was charged with common assault and given a court date for the following year. My parents' tendency to act like bad things didn't happen meant they never reprimanded me for it. In fact, it was never mentioned again. It also meant they didn't ask if I was mentally okay or why I'd been suddenly, uncharacteristically violent. Instead, they just worked hard to act like the court case wasn't happening.

My defence lawyer read out statements from the others who'd been at the party. It was surreal hearing other people's perspective on what happened but it sounded pretty accurate.

'Going through the statements in front of me here . . . It's like trying to untangle something out of a soap opera.'

He picked up a piece of paper and squinted through his glasses, reading with the weariness of a guy who had been doing this for too long. ' "Everything was fine then Fern just stood up and hit her out of nowhere." ' He peered over his glasses at me.

I nodded. 'Yeah, pretty much. She was going to hit me first, so I had to.'

He leaned back in his chair. 'You were drinking at this party . . .'

This was said less as a question, more as an assertion of fact, but I shook my head immediately. 'No, I don't drink.'

'But you'd had a drink.'

'No, I hadn't had anything to drink.'

He looked at me for a moment. 'But you must have had something?'

Is this guy stupid?

I sighed. 'No.'

'Because they'd be more lenient if you *had* . . .'

'I told you: I don't really like drinking.'

He put his head in his hands. My inability to read between the lines or lie led to me being fined £200. I'm told autistic people in prison regularly fail their parole meetings when asked if they regret what they've done, as they answer honestly, 'No' – whereas allistics understand the social rewards that come with lying and saying the 'correct' thing even when they don't mean it.

I acquired a girlfriend within a month of being at university. She was a kind languages student from Yorkshire who was continually trying to sort out my money and life problems since I was apparently incapable of doing so myself. We'd been together a couple of months when we went out to celebrate me not going to prison (though quietly, I still felt fairly sure these were my final months on the outside).

I bumped into John in a nightclub called Opium in

the Cowgate. John was the best-looking guy around by a mile. Mum used to go on about how gorgeous he was. She said he looked like an angel. He wasn't even good-looking in a Bathgate way, which was a relative type of good looks where you had to throw normal standards out the window 'cause most of the men looked like big raw hams.

I'd actually seen him the other week working in the Tesco near our Edinburgh flat but had been too shy to speak to him properly. I'd been staring at the bakery shelf one day and he'd appeared behind the rows of baguettes. Like a vision. I love bread so the effect of seeing him surrounded by it was intoxicating.

That night, I ended up leaving my girlfriend at her place to let John and his brother in to stay at our flat across the road. They lived in Leith and it was too far to get back to, they said; but I only had a single bed so we let his brother sleep there while we stayed up talking all night in the living room next door. I fancied John so much it was hard to speak or move without feeling crippling self-consciousness. I felt like I was going to faint when I was around him, which I'd never felt before and haven't since. I still don't know if that was a good thing. At 5am he finally kissed me and fell asleep on my shoulder while reruns of *Friends* looped on the TV. I was sitting as still as possible so I didn't wake him up as I knew Callie would come into the living room at 6am for her early-morning law lecture. When she saw the sleeping male model on my shoulder, I beamed at her silently and tried not to look smug. A conventionally attractive boyfriend was a generic achievement we could all understand and it seemed everyone valued shagging a boyfriend rather than a stranger.

John's brother came through later that morning and said to me bluntly, 'Your bedroom's fucking disgusting.' John found this hilarious. After they left, I felt so happy that John had kissed me I glossed over the thing with his brother pretty quickly.

We arranged to go on a date the following weekend. I went into my overdraft to buy a first-date outfit. I didn't know what an overdraft was because no one had told me but from what I could gauge it seemed to be some sort of free money the banks gave as a present to students and I'd managed to acquire two or three with different banks in addition to several store credit cards that I used to buy food when I ran out of overdraft money. I waited in my bedroom looking at my phone every two minutes. Eventually, I fell asleep on top of my duvet, still in my new clothes. John had stood me up.

Apparently, he had forgotten, so we set up another date. We went to this underground pub with an empty cinema in one of Edinburgh's dungeon-y cellars. Some terrible film where Jennifer Aniston owns a pet ferret played on a loop while we kissed and kissed and kissed. He wouldn't have sex with me on our first few dates. But when I was drunk – like, mad drunk, falling-down drunk – we did.

I never understood the appeal of having sex when you're drunk: it's numbing, it's sloppy and it feels like the alcohol is being used as an excuse to ignore the sex. Now I'm in my thirties, I wonder if men do this because they're frightened of women laughing at their sexual performance or being better than them. And so they need them to be drunk.

And yet, it felt magical to meet someone who didn't have the same boring version of masculinity that involved being semi-literate and knocking lumps out of other men every weekend. He had the same accent as me but the same intellect and curiosity about the world and culture too. There was no one like that at school and no one like that at university. At school, everyone had the same accent as me but was thick. At university everyone loved to read and learn but since I was one of the despised locals, they treated me as if I'd just crawled out of a cave on all fours. After a few months surrounded by these students I couldn't tell anymore if I was the weird one for growing up without a butler or a nanny. With him around, we could laugh at people having swimming pools and helicopters and not knowing the price of anything.

Defining yourself as the girlfriend of someone impressive was easier than working out who you were or what version of impressive you should be, especially if you're a weird woman.

My housemate in the room next to me pounded the walls one night, yelling plummily, 'Do you two *ever* stop shagging?' Another night, she and Callie came home drunk and knocked on our door giggling to tell us off, so he answered it naked.

I asked my year tutor if she could give me a reference of good character in my upcoming court case for assault. She said no and pointed out that I'd attended precisely three classes all semester; but it was her mask of quiet horror that made me realize this sort of request didn't come up a lot among Edinburgh's trust-fund kids. I'd attended one Persian class and all I could say in Farsi was, 'My sister has a pomegranate.' The tutor had assured us: 'You will need this. Pomegranates are integral to Iranian society.' I asked the university if I could switch to an English lit degree, believing that this might make me feel less like I've felt from nursery through to high school and now university – that being around a lot of new people in a new place is too much to bear. When my request was accepted for the following year I spent the rest of the academic year working (and getting sacked from) every bar in the Cowgate in between spending every other waking moment with John.

From early on in our relationship, we did whatever he wanted as I still couldn't believe I was going out with someone so attractive. I desperately wanted to please him because I'd a terrible gnawing feeling I'd get found out soon and he'd realize how crap I was.

We had to play pool for hours and hours. If I ever said I wanted to go home after the tenth or twentieth game, he'd lie on the floor of the student union pretending to have learning difficulties or a seizure to embarrass me into continuing.

Now that I didn't have coursework to do, all we did was play pool while he went on and on about the same stuff. John barely went back to his own flat anymore and once he ran out of clean clothes would simply wear mine, stretching my T-shirts over his 6-foot frame. I liked it; it added to the sense we were turning into one person and that was what all the books and magazines said you should want.

'Catholics believe in transubstantiation, you know. They believe the Communion literally turns into Jesus' flesh.'

'Yeah, I know,' I said meekly. He brought up how stupid our beliefs in transubstantiation were every day but I'd never heard the word until I met him. Neither my grandparents nor my parents nor anyone at school mentioned it.

'It's so *stupid*,' he continued, shaking his head.

'I know. I'm an atheist too,' I replied, thinking how only a year ago I'd been insisting to my parents that Catholicism was stupid and now I had a Protestant telling me the same thing.

'They believe in *papal infallibility*.'

I sighed, irritated that I was 'them' and couldn't help it. 'I already don't believe in this.'

He shook his head and continued. I felt as though it was better to let him go on as all he wanted was a silent audience. He'd rotate through transubstantiation, Catholic stupidity, scientists' superiority, the unparalleled genius of Richard Dawkins and how he was drafting a letter of complaint to some evangelical-Christian organization. Then he'd read the letter out proudly. I'd smile and nod and agree how clever and funny he was before he moved on to one of his other favourite topics. These were mostly, if not always, limited to one of the following subjects:

The genius of Mahler's *Das Lied von der Erde*
The life of the Italian Baroque painter Caravaggio
The life of snooker champion Alex 'Hurricane' Higgins
Stravinsky's *The Rite of Spring*

Occasionally he'd take a break from these topics to put on some weird timelapse arthouse film called *Koyaanisqatsi* and bellow along: 'KOYAANISQATSI!'

'Can we watch something else? I still have Callie's *Legally Blonde* DVD?'

'KOYAANISQATSI!'

I was always the audience for him and his opinions. I once

watched him dance shirtless in front of a mirror in his flat while *The Rite of Spring* blasted on the record player. I had been waiting for us to go out before inevitably returning to my flat. He was then back onto Caravaggio again.

'Caravaggio killed a man, you know,' he said, out of breath. He danced faster as the music sped up. 'And he got away with it.' He danced faster and faster, doing weird jerky puppet movements, staring at himself in the mirror.

I liked how eccentric he was. He felt like my twin, albeit the more popular, confident one. Adam, my ex-boyfriend in high school, had been eccentric but unsure of himself. John made big sweeping statements all the time and was devastatingly funny with an offbeat sense of humour. The girls in the student flat all loved to be around him. Everyone loved him. Everyone except Lauren.

I was laughing at something she'd texted me one day as I sat beside him on the couch.

'She's not as funny as you think, you know.' He said it casually, eyes not moving away from the TV, but to say Lauren wasn't funny was such sacrilege the barb caught me.

'What do you mean?'

'You make out she's hilarious, but she's not that funny.'

I woke up at John's parents' house on Boxing Day. We'd only been seeing each other a couple of months. I felt shy at first as my family would never in a million years let me have someone I wasn't married to stay over, but they were Protestants so my presence at breakfast in the morning was as mundane as going to the toilet. They invited me to stay all day and have dinner with them. His sister was there with her partner and their baby. They had a huge Rottweiler that, like all owners of huge Rottweilers do, they insisted was friendly.

As I walked up their driveway his dad booted a football towards me. As with all sports, I froze and stood motionless watching it dopily. The ball hit me in the vag.

'Oof! Right in the fanny!' The dad, John and his brother all laughed to each other. Protestants were nuts, man. Everyone was so casual with each other.

John turned to me: 'We play a family game every Boxing Day where we take turns going through the alphabet and saying a swear word for each letter.'

I nodded, grateful for the heads-up.

Throughout dinner and drinks and Christmas telly, I remained deep in thought about how I could win the swearing game and everyone's hearts and minds. Finally, the game started and I watched them go round the assembled siblings and their respective partners.

His mother said, 'Arsehole.'

Grinning, his dad said, 'Bastard.'

I watched the baby play with the Rottweiler. His sister chirped, 'Cock!'

Mentally, I tried to work out what my letters would be for each of my turns. I said something weak for my first word but finally it came to me again. If I wanted to make this family love me, I needed to impress them with something spectacular. I paused, smiling shyly down at the floor before looking up to play my trump card: 'Munter!'

'Oh?' someone said. 'What *is* a munter?'

'Well, actually, the practice of munting is – I mean, what I've read anyway – is when two men go to a graveyard, dig up a body – um, usually female – and then they take turns jumping up and down on its stomach while the other one puts their dick in its mouth and then, uh, the sensation of the intestines slopping up into the corpse's mouth is meant to be quite . . . quite pleasurable?'

I grinned. I'd passed their Protestant filth test with flying colours. I felt like Princess Diana must have felt when she was first invited to Balmoral and made the Royal Family love her by shooting a stag.

No one spoke for a moment. Some people were shaking their heads in disbelief; some were smirking at the floor.

The dad went, 'Well. Fucking hell. Who'd have thought. Whose turn is it?'

The sister's husband volunteered: 'Nipples.' They all nodded approvingly. I stared at the floor and wished I'd gone for something as boring as nipples.

That night, John shut the door to the spare room behind him. My face peeked out from under the quilt on the sofa bed.

'I can't believe you said that to my parents.' He laughed, shaking his head and making the same confusing face the others had made at me earlier. I wished I didn't have to see them all again in the morning.

'How was I supposed to know not to say that in a swearing game?'

'How were you supposed to know not to mention necrophilia at Christmas dinner?'

I turned over and stared at the wall. Trying to make people like you was an impossible code I would never crack.

I relayed the incident to my brother when I was back at our parents' house the next day.

'Well, how *could* you know? They play a swearing game at Christmas – what even *is* that?'

Exactly, I nodded. It wasn't me that was the problem. You didn't know where you were with Proddies. Their social codes were so awry.

I remembered then a time at my ex-boyfriend Adam's house where his dad had said, 'Get my breakfast ready – I'm off to see these cunts down the golf club.' The use of 'cunt' in Scotland is interchangeable with 'person' or 'people'. For example, 'good cunt' is an informal term for someone who's an all-round great guy. A 'daft cunt' is a silly person. The way Adam's dad had just used it was in a tone that implied 'these guys' or the French *mes amis*. Of course, I didn't yet know that the tonality of 'cunt' in Scottish vernacular was as complex as Mandarin because my parents never swore in front of us. So that morning, when Adam dropped the toast butter-side down, I – ever eager to fit in with the family's social codes – shouted gleefully, 'Don't drop the toast, you stupid cunt!' Immediately his dad spun on his heel to face me. I didn't like Adam's dad.

'Listen to me now. Never. Ever. Speak like that to any of my family again. Got that?'

I nodded, cringing under his stare. I thought I was doing the right thing by joining the family's social codes and calling everyone a cunt. But you couldn't *actually* call someone a cunt. Calling someone a cunt was calling someone a cunt no matter where you were. Unless they were a good cunt, in which case you were fine. It felt pointless to get As in language classes at school when there seemed to be this whole other secret language no one was telling you about that relied on instincts I didn't have.

Nowadays, I find Scottish sectarianism comically parochial but my parents, grandparents and school had it drilled into us from day one. I kept categorizing all this odd behaviour from boyfriends' families into 'must be Protestants', overlooking the fact that I didn't fit in with Catholic social norms either. I didn't fit in anywhere.

Chapter Seven

'Making fear memories permanent helps animals to survive in the wild. The ones that forget where they met a lion will not survive.'

—Temple Grandin, *Thinking in Pictures*

I moved out of student accommodation at the end of the academic year, owing thousands in unpaid rent, and into John's flat in Leith. He lived with a weird guy who read a book on Buddhism after his divorce and subsequently gave away all his possessions and most of their furniture shortly before I moved in. As a result we slept on a mattress in the living room. John insisted that our 'floor bed' was far superior to a normal bed and we should appreciate it. Some poor guy tried to burgle us but left with only an ancient jacket – there was little to no demand on Leith's black market for Mahler records and English lit textbooks.

We had to move to a flat on Ferry Road. John taught me how to make scrambled eggs in a big frying pan so they cooked quicker. He told me art was the closest thing we had to being able to see inside other people's brains.

For the first year of the relationship I was drunk on shagging this ten when I knew I was a six. And, it should be pointed out, drunk on drink. My dad left my mum around this time and the shock made me sick to my stomach so I stopped eating as often.

I have very few memories of spending time with friends or family during this period, and university life faded into the background, as my number-one preoccupation became the relationship.

John and I split up. I had to move back in with my mum, and then she kicked me out too.

As I packed my stuff, in what was now such a well-worn routine it felt like pantomime, I realized: *It's my twentieth birthday today* . . .

I went out in Edinburgh that night, too embarrassed to tell any of my friends that I was homeless. I couldn't think of a way to turn it into a joke and figured if I didn't say it out loud it would be less real.

I tried to make myself feel better by kissing some guy in a nightclub, hoping I could stay at his place, but he ran away from me as soon as we got outside, which was truly the perfect ending to this ridiculous birthday.

I stayed at my uncle's council flat in Leith.

John showed up at the flat. We argued, I hid in the toilet and shat non-stop as I was now abusing laxatives for reasons that remain a mystery to me.

I'd decided to only eat cornflakes now. Less stressful to stick to one food.

I went out to some Czech bar at the top of Leith Walk and pulled a caveman-y guy, relieved not to have to make conversation. At the time, I preferred guys with limited English as this eliminated the need for small talk and reduced conversation to its most functional: 'You have flat? I come back?'

My uncle returned to the flat and told me I had to leave as his girlfriend had dumped him and he needed the place back. I couldn't go back to my mum's and I had no idea where my dad had gone.

I looked for homeless services in Edinburgh but all I could find was a service for homeless dogs. I booked into the same backpackers' hostel in the West End that I'd stayed in when I was 18 and was amazed at how calm I felt.

I went to the supermarket near the hostel, thinking, *Buy a toothbrush, buy shower gel, buy toothpaste* . . . Then I wondered whether I was supposed to buy food and felt overwhelmed at the choice and decided against it. Everything was objectively VERY BAD but I felt calm and didn't need to eat.

I went to the payphone in the street and phoned John. He didn't answer. I hung up and tried to think what to do.

At the hostel I met some lads from Cork who told me their friend had a flat in Leith with cheap rooms. I moved in within days and was incredulous I finally had my own bedroom.

There was a really blissful couple of months where I was properly skinny for the first and only time in my life and I was going out with my Kiwi flatmates and riding guys with impunity and walking around naked with confidence.

I subsequently became friends with, and started dating, a grungy 30-year-old who was gorgeous and severely bipolar and whose dick didn't work because he was on a cocktail of antipsychotics.

I booked in to do resit exams at university, hoping this would mean I didn't mess up my first year for a second time.

I still hadn't worked out how everyone else seemed to just *know* how to do university life. After almost two years in this place, I still didn't understand the process for submitting essays (I hadn't written any, since I couldn't really use computers or word-processing software); I had no idea which buildings were which and no idea who to ask for help. I'd missed multiple exams as I didn't know how to find out what building they were in – and even if I'd found that out, I didn't know what books I was supposed to be looking at to revise in a library I didn't know how to use. Even if I could have got help, I didn't have the language to say what the problem was. All I felt was a suffocating horror that I was failing at being clever, which couldn't possibly be the case because all my parents and teachers had ever told me was how very clever I was.

I made an earnest attempt at revising for my resits, still feeling unsure of how to even tackle the thing.

'You look like a ballerina,' said the grungy guy as I lankily stepped over tables in a bar to get off with him.

Then John came back. 'You look like a giraffe,' he said as I wobbled towards him on heels, 20lbs lighter than before. We went to a bar, supposedly to have tentative talks about getting back together; we ended up kissing and the heat in my stomach made me think I was never going to break up with him.

The following day I started my resits. I sat and stared into space, completely forgetting that I was in an exam hall and writing nothing on the exam paper for an exam I hadn't revised for because all I could think about was John.

By this point it was August and the Edinburgh Festival Fringe. John and I went to watch an obnoxiously alpha-male stand-up comedian and afterwards I said, 'I could do that.' John laughed and assured me it was much harder than it looked. 'But I could do that,' I said again. 'That guy was just shouting stuff about his dick on stage.' He ignored me and gave me a piggyback and we shout-sang the *Home and Away* theme tune, 'You know we belong together/You and I forever and ever . . .' as we crashed down South Bridge.

Within days I didn't want to be back with him. I decided to end it decisively, once and for all, by doing something that would make sure he definitely wouldn't come near me ever again. After we had got back together again, he passed out drunk next to me one night. I took his phone and called his ex who he was still friends with (the one who hated me) and told her he was always cheating on her. He woke up to a flurry of calls and frantic texts from her. It was the middle of the night. As he realized what I'd done his facial expression turned cold. Every muscle in my body stiffened as I instinctively geared up for whatever was coming next. I didn't yet know how bad it was going to be. He silently picked up my phone, bending it in his hands, hands shaking under the pressure. The phone gave in, snapping in two. He took smaller parts of it out and snapped them in half too. I noticed then, with some alarm, that his arms – which were normally pretty thin – had gotten bigger and stronger over the summer. He picked up my CDs and DVDs, snapping them one by one.

I don't remember speaking but I remember sitting up in bed before he flung me back, spitting in my face. Before I knew what was happening I felt him crawl on top of me and bite down hard into my cheek. He was biting my nose. He was definitely biting my nose. *This is happening.* I wondered if he'd take chunks out. It occurred to me right that second that I was almost definitely in a toxic relationship.

He strangled me for a bit before spitting on me again. Then, with his face looming over me, I saw the pillow slowly move across his features like an eclipse. Time sped up again as the pillow clamped down onto my face like a full stop. *Oh, I see. I see what you're doing here*, I thought.

I was totally incredulous. I really had not anticipated dying this way. This was not on-brand for me. If I was going to die young I wanted to at least kill myself or something. Domestic abuse happened to, like, women that aren't at university. *EastEnders*. It happened in *EastEnders* to shrieking oppressed wives with no agency, not to sassy women like me.

The pillow was still on my face.

I couldn't breathe.

I felt mortified at the thought of my flatmates finding my dead body.

The pillow was still on my face.

I felt a bit sad.

I felt calm.

The pillow came off my face with a big *whooosh* as the air rushed back into my lungs. I blinked at the light. John was sobbing. I felt embarrassed for him. Unsure of how to respond to this new John, the one who wanted to kill me, I shakily started to cry too. I wasn't sure what I was crying about but it seemed safest just to mirror him until I could work out what to do next.

'Why did you do this?' he sobbed into the pillow. 'I came here tonight to tell you I fucking *love you*. I was gonna ask you to *marry me*.'

I thought, *Are you fucking kidding*? I started to cry harder as I was sad then and sad because as much as I loved the idea of the 'crazy-writer-goes-out-with-eccentric' trope, I didn't have this in mind. Not even close.

I was terrified but leaving didn't seem like an option. In the morning I had no idea what to say. He said he would buy me a new phone. I can't remember how I got this message without a mobile and without Facebook having been invented yet but somehow Lauren reminded me we were going to a talk by the author Jeanette Winterson at the Edinburgh Book Festival.

Dazed, I left the house unshowered and made my way up Leith Walk to the posh side of town, to George Square Gardens and the marquees of authors.

I had an evangelical experience at the Jeanette Winterson reading. She talked about when her mum destroyed all her beloved books in a fire and she realized that art is a good thing because you carry it with you inside after.

I cried or the tears got stuck in my throat, I'm not sure. Winterson grew up in working-class Lancashire and at the talk she said: 'When students complain now about money and ask how I did it I say, "You just had to work bloody hard."'

I mulled this over, wondering how much longer I could

avoid paying rent and eke out a living with the £80-a-month grant and stealing from the bookies I was working in. Just work bloody hard.

Weeks later, Lauren would tell me that I hadn't been acting right at the event. I had zero recollection of this. She said I'd seemed dazed afterwards, and had told her, 'I have to go. I still have spit in my hair,' before walking off without saying bye.

That night, after I saw Jeanette Winterson, John turned up at my flat with a new phone for me and was initially hugely apologetic then angry again. We argued over me ringing his ex.

I went back into my bedroom and looked at the floor.

I couldn't work out why the carpet appeared to be glittering all over.

I lifted my gaze and from the door to the window were sparkly shards of CDs and DVDs he'd broken over and over again.

Bruises appeared on my arms and nose.

A mouth-shaped bruise appeared on my cheek.

I walked into the living room and asked my flatmate if she would go to the police station with me.

I started my first year at university for the third time, having failed my resit exams. Standing in the hallway of the English lit department to see which tutorial group I was in, I chatted briefly to another student and it came up that I was doing my first year for the third time. She looked at me doubtfully. Her 'Oh, good luck?' was humiliating enough to ensure I became an overachiever for the next decade or so.

I studied every night, my landlord regularly forgot to collect rent, my Kiwi flatmates were easy-going and quietly protective over me after the attack and life was good. There was a weird eerie sort of silence in my head. It felt like someone had put noise-cancelling headphones on my inner monologue. John had been charged with common assault and malicious mischief, a Scottish charge that's so peculiarly olden-days-sounding that I couldn't take it seriously. The police took a statement but I didn't cry until they took pictures of my injuries – it was only then that I realized they were real.

The police put a restraining order in place. I was forced to tell my course tutor about the court case so I'd be allowed to stay on at university having failed my exams. They referred me to the university counselling service who – in my first and only session with them – heard 'My boyfriend tried to kill me with a pillow' and made me a stammering referral to a psychiatrist. There were a lot of referrals after that, mainly just to get me out of people's offices as I was making them uncomfortable. I realized later that this discomfort came from the fact I wasn't performing the role of victim correctly – saying, 'My boyfriend put a pillow on my face,' in a flat, disaffected tone was unnerving to most folk and may have led the university staff to the conclusion that I was insane rather than traumatized. Or they just fucked up.

I would smile sitting on the top deck of the bus as I glided through town to my regular psychiatric appointments at the Royal Edinburgh Hospital, the passengers getting more wild-eyed and less genteel as we moved from Brunswick through to Morningside. The appointments were less than useless as the psychiatrist was there to medicate a normal response to the trauma of being violently attacked but it was nice to talk to someone, I guess.

Trying to explain my sense of having a brand-new life – something I believe is common in women whose boyfriends have recently tried to smother them – I told the (male) psychiatrist I felt almost euphoric and he started a line of questioning I recognized as trying to diagnose a manic phase. When he asked if I felt delusions of grandeur I realized where he was going with this.

'I'm not manic,' I said, and smiled non-manically.

'I think I might have Asperger's,' I told him one day. I'd been mulling it over for a few years and finally had the confidence to say it to a doctor.

The psychiatrist shook his head immediately, chuckling at the ridiculousness of my suggestion. This was when I was told I didn't fit the criteria because I was making eye contact and I'd had boyfriends.

At the time, my faith in doctors and their absolute infallibility was so all-encompassing I felt stupid for even mentioning it, what with my incredible eye contact – this eye contact that he believed would carry me through life.

I was also having good sex with an Estonian lad who I'd met in a hellish Australian-themed nightclub. It was a great arrangement and best of all he didn't question why I couldn't sleep in the bed with him after; the bed where it happened. Instead, I'd leave him to sleep and go through to my kitchen, crouching on the floor to try and relieve the cramps tearing through my stomach. I made no connection to the fact that this twisting and tearing was now happening every time I was alone with a man. Without even realizing it, it was around about then that I stopped going out with anyone physically bigger or taller than me.

I phoned Mum and tried my best to have a civil conversation with her.

'Fern, was John in an advert for Napier Uni?'

'No,' I said, wondering why she'd bring up the person I have a restraining order against as if it was fun chit-chat.

'Are you sure? Did he maybe dye his hair brown for the advert?'

'He's not in an advert.'

'Well, this guy is the double of him. Oh! Oh! This guy was wearing a ring. Does John wear a ring?'

I thought that I'd maybe like to not talk about John. The biting and the spit and the pillow coming over my face played in my head, like a video caught in a loop.

I didn't tell her that, though; instead I offered abruptly: 'I've been getting therapy at the Royal Ed.'

She scoffed. 'Why do *you* need therapy?'

I said nothing.

I can't remember who got in touch with who first. It had to have been me. It can't have been me. But we got back together and he was apologetic and so was I – I was very sorry I caused this – and we cried and I giggled and hid him under the bed when my special liaison officer came over to give me updates on the case. I felt the whimsical young love narrative move further and further out of my view.

John told me he'd never be able to teach. And of course I said I'd write a letter to the court for him, asking the judge to be lenient.

I poured all my effort into the letter instead of my university essay on Euripides and compiled two or three pages.

John's charge was reduced to a breach of the peace.

That's a loud party.

The worst thing that's ever happened to me was on a par with a loud party.

He was fined £200.

Outside the court, my case officer looked at me then looked to John lurking in the background.

'Please don't tell me you're back with him?'

I nodded slowly, mortified at my life, and he shook his head in disgust.

I was disgusted with myself.

John said he didn't try to kill me.

Shortly after this it was our anniversary. I made a disgusting monkfish in vermouth dish that I couldn't afford and John said nothing and we both took a load of speed and insulted each other.

I tried to write about what happened as I still couldn't believe it. The scene played out over and over again in my head and none of my friends seemed to know what to say when I tried to speak to them about it.

I took all my Prozac and all my painkillers.

*

This is incredibly common in women who've been attacked by their partner.

Trying to kill yourself never pans out the way it does in films. In hospital they do ask you if you meant to kill yourself but it's such a factual box-ticking exercise that to answer with any kind of emotion would be mortifying. There's no 'It was a cry for help' box but there should be.

I feel like the doctors and the general public need to raise awareness of how embarrassing most suicide attempts are. When you're in a backless hospital gown with your worst pants on it's really hard to hold your nerve and say, 'I wanted to die.'

Any overdose scenario I've had has gone like this:

Doctor: 'Did you want to hurt yourself?'
Patient: 'No, I *[looking at doctor, hoping they see the hidden pain]* just took every tablet in my house by mistake.'
Doctor: 'Great, we'll get a nurse to discharge you.'

I was told I wasn't going to die. And John left.

In the morning I sat in bed waiting for someone who'd tell me not to kill myself again. No one came.

An old man was repeatedly leaving his bed and wandering off, then being occasionally guided back by a harried nurse.

I swang my legs off the bed and headed out.

Chapter Eight

'You fondle my trigger then you blame my gun'

—Fiona Apple, 'Limp'

'Did stripping make you hate men?' a guy asked me ten years after I had stopped.

The question implied that stripping had clouded my judgement and made me a grizzled hag gazing angrily into the middle distance rather than giving me perfect clarity over the fact that the world hates women. Before #MeToo, before Time's Up, before feminism's fourth wave – before any of it – I knew, and it was one of the best things that I could have learned as a young woman. Arguably, men made me hate men; stripping just let me see them at their most men-ish.

I saw this really great comedian on TV once saying: 'Strippers always brag that "the men can't touch us . . ."' She smiled before delivering her punchline. 'Yes, well, that's true of *any* workplace.' The crowd laughed, the laughter indicating that, 'Yes, we all agree strippers are stupid.' *Those* women are stupid. *Those* women think they're not oppressed. The othering of sex workers gives all the good girls a boost, something that helps them feel like *their* lives, *their* notions of behaving respectably, *their* gender performance, *their* church weddings and the subsequent thanklessness of unpaid childcare is somehow okay; rewarding, even. It's an elegant piece of stand-up that made me laugh in spite of myself but, as the #MeToo movement revealed, it's woefully inaccurate. Women *do* get groped in the workplace and are too ashamed to say anything 'cause normal workplaces keep up the pretence that women are equal to their male colleagues. The bind is this: I've never lost jobs in a strip club for speaking out about male harassment. We had no shame in calling men out in the clubs. Instead, we just had the offensive man immediately removed by a big Latvian bouncer on steroids. How many women can say the same in Hollywood, comedy, the media, the music industry or any number of professions that have had their own sexual-harassment scandals? When there are no clearly marked boundaries then a man's transgression is made so much simpler. As a young woman in stand-up there was a pretence that I was on the same level as my male counterparts, that it was all a meritocracy rewarded by hard work and talent, and so I just had to put the blinkers on and not complain.

Part of autistic survival is learning to unpick social dynamics. I liked that in a strip club men's contempt of you was out in the open. In the outside world, misogyny was always hovering in your peripheral vision, meaning you could never quite trust your instincts. In a strip club, groups of men are in a safe space where they're encouraged to play up to hypermasculine ideals – and because they believe no one in power is watching them they project all their shame and irregular feelings about women onto the strippers, who they believe exist in a vacuum and won't ever speak out about their behaviour or, say, write about it in a tell-all memoir.

No one ever asks me about the men.

All they ever want to know about is the naked bit. People have a hard time getting their head round the naked part when it's the least interesting thing about the job. Me, I've never been a naked person. I do not get changed in front of other women (I've tried; the forced casualness feels insane) and I do not go into the same toilet cubicle with other women on nights out. My parents used to chastise me if my jumper lifted up and they could see an inch of 'my big bare back', as my dad called it. But when your nakedness is a uniform it becomes normal.

I didn't realize how at odds my views on stripping were with everyone else's until it came to writing a script on the topic. I really wanted to write about the nature of outsiders. I wrote about the dull repetitiveness of the job and of sitting on couches in my underwear night after night watching TV and chatting to interesting women about every topic under the sun while we waited for customers to come in. Over and over again I was told people didn't get it. One script editor said repeatedly, 'Why would anyone become a stripper?' leading me to have to awkwardly mention I had done it and that – crazy, I know – I did it because I needed a lot of money and didn't have any.

I was told (by male commissioners) that I wasn't showing

sufficient shame, that I was intellectualizing my past experiences to hide the secret pain I felt. I burst into tears with frustration during one meeting as I'd started to realize they wanted some emotional response I didn't have. I completely understand objectively that it's a shameful job and that, in line with society's story about how women are meant to feel about themselves, I'm supposed to feel negatively about it; but I've experienced a lot of unusual situations in life objectively, similar to watching a film or reading a novel.

Most people are so clueless and uncomfortable talking to me about my old job that they can barely look me in the eye. The silence around it is why I love being around other strippers or ex-strippers. There's a shorthand to it. A couple of years ago I met a Glaswegian dominatrix who started off working in the same clubs as me. We reminisced about the places we'd worked and whether we knew the same people. I told her the problems I was having with explaining to TV producers what I saw as a simple idea about stripping. She shook her head like she'd heard it before. 'You have to understand, with a lot of these people, they're projecting their own feelings of shame onto you.'

There was a lot of that.

'I wouldn't do that,' a girl I'd never met before said to me at a Hogmanay party. I was sitting on the floor opposite her, ashtrays and bottles of Glen's vodka round about us. She looked at the little circle of people on the couches, addressing them as well as me. 'I just couldnae do something like that.' She looked at me ruefully, like I was a threat. I rubbed my hands against the fibre of the carpet and stayed quiet. I was getting used to the uncomfortable symbolic function my job now served for people. It was the same at university and on the student newspaper. Everyone suddenly became very interested in studying the walls if I mentioned my job but was magically able to phone me up and ask me directly about it the second they had an internship at a big newspaper and promised their editor they could do a piece on Edinburgh's secret sleaze.

My mum didn't find out till a few years ago. She was scanning shopping through the checkouts at Tesco and excitedly saw a review of one of my shows where I had mentioned stripping accidentally, blurting it out in a panic while trying new material on stage. Some slavering journalist had decided to print it.

'Is it true?' she said shakily on the phone to me during her break. 'What would your brothers say?'

She did not ask me whether I had found it stressful. Her primary concern was focused on whether or not I was an embarrassment to the community and our family.

I first discovered the notion of autistic strippers when I was filling out my assessment forms back when I was first diagnosed and came across the work of writer and stripper Reece Piper. Reading about why stripping is appealing to some autistic women, I realized there was more than one of us. Thinking back over some of my old workmates, there were possibly even loads of us. My pragmatic views made sense: of course I enjoyed a job that was highly tolerant of weirdos, almost impossible to get sacked from, had none of the fluorescent lighting that made most offices or supermarket jobs overwhelming, involved the same routine night after night and the same dumb conversations with men with no tricky social cues to read. I feel like people who are outside of autism but autism-adjacent – parents, carers, therapists – would like to say that autistic women end up in sex work because we're vulnerable and easily taken advantage of. That may well be true for some but to say it's the only reason is to deny us our agency, to deny the fact that we found the one job that incidentally has all the reasonable adaptations lacking in most office environments and that we did what was best for ourselves in harsh circumstances. I'm never going to say it's empowering; I put paid to that idea after I had to bicker with a girl over which of us got to dress as a sexy schoolgirl on costume night.

All stripping is, as any sex work is, brutally honest about the transactional dynamic that exists between a lot of men and women. Allistic people are uncomfortable with this. Women need the idea of romance to make them change their surnames to their male owner's name, a tradition that's rooted in oppression and that many educated women continue with anyway. Women still ignore the fact that pregnancy and childbirth make them financially vulnerable. Many TV shows are still hosted by an old man and a young or young-seeming thin woman. Even serious news journalists are forced to fit into the same doll-like template for all women in broadcasting. Panel shows are still filled with ugly, overweight male comedians then the woman comedian's spot is filled by a model or pretty reality TV star whose function is ornamental. She's there to laugh at the men but mostly she's there because she's conventionally attractive. Whether the industry wants to admit it to itself or not, there is a tacit understanding in TV that the prettiest, thinnest, blondest woman will get the work. Now tell me: how is any of this different to a strip club?

The seed was planted when I picked up a student newspaper on campus. There was a girl in a negligee on the cover, smiling knowingly into the camera. She had one leg wrapped around a pole and was wearing Perspex heels. The headline read: 'STUDENTS STRIPPED FOR CASH'.

The subhead to this supposedly cautionary leader bragged: 'I make up to £300 a night lap dancing!' I read the story over and over again. I ended up meeting at least three others who went into stripping as a result of seeing that article, all of them students.

I was still working in a bookies in Leith but my manager was increasingly too drunk to function and the place tended towards chaos more often than not. We had to barricade ourselves in the office after a guy foamed at the mouth and tried to smash the door in with a fire extinguisher. As I struggled to both hold the door shut and dial 999 while watching him generate an almost unbelievable amount of foam, it occurred to me that this was categorized as a non-degrading job. I had become increasingly aware that I was having a good-looking year. I was still thin. Plus I had a lot more time on my hands now. The stripper article was still on my bookshelf. After I'd reread it several times and rehearsed what I was going to say, I phoned up the club mentioned and arranged to come in for an audition – though I'd no idea what that'd entail. I went to see a uni friend, to tell him I was going to go work in a strip club. He was working in an internet cafe.

'Stripping's your first step on the ladder to prostitution,' he said confidently. He was always making neat confident statements on stuff about me.

Christ knows what I wore to the audition but I think it was soft-pink matching underwear, the kind you buy to surprise your on-off boyfriend in the hope he won't strangle you again.

Living in Edinburgh, a city with seven strip clubs at its peak in the early noughties, I was used to seeing the girls outside smoking in the doorways in long coats – but everyone knows you just walk past those places hurriedly and try not to even look in their direction. I dunno why you try and avoid looking at them 'cause you don't want to be tainted by it. I was fully not prepared for what greeted me when I went in.

We all generally have a photofit in our head of what a strip-club boss looks like. Tony Soprano. Peter Stringfellow. Maybe balding with a greasy ponytail and a leather jacket. Crucially they'll have a sort of sleazy sneer that underlines their contempt for the vacant fembots working for them.

Jim looked like a maths teacher or a kindly uncle. He wore short-sleeved checked shirts, had a thatch of grey hair, little round glasses and a cheerful face that wouldn't have looked out of place in a Santa costume. (There's no big reveal down the line, where Jim is actually a rapist or a bad bastard. To this day I have no idea how he ended up in strip clubs and not running a Rotary Club.)

Jim used to run the club with a much nastier guy called Dougie who had died the week I joined. On one of my very first shifts a load of strippers wearing black and in sunglasses walked into the bar sniffling and dabbing their eyes after attending Dougie's funeral. I wanted to ask them what had happened but I was still at this point frightened of 90 per cent of strippers, plus one or two were giving those heavy 'fuck off' vibes common from those who've been drinking after a funeral.

Seeing such a bizarre sight so early on was one of the things that made me want to stay. If that seems callous to the grieving girls muttering through the tears that 'Dougie was the best', I met an equal number of girls who'd hiss, 'Dougie was a cunt,' before staring into the middle distance and refusing to say any more on the matter. Dougie wasn't just a standard bad strip-club boss in the sense that he'd steal your money or fine you for made-up reasons. He *was*, by many accounts anyway, a serial rapist. But I found that out much later on from a close friend. I really wish I hadn't as it made me realize my guilelessness was a delusion and it was only by chance that I'd been left untouched.

'So!' Jim pushed his glasses up his nose and beamed at me. 'Since you've never been to a strip club before, Elena will give you a lap dance to show you how it's done and then you can dance for me and then we can have a chat and go through any questions. Okay?'

I nodded brightly as if it was a trial shift at an upmarket cafe. Before I knew it Elena, a Greek girl with a swooshy black bob, had sat me down and was swinging her big boobs in my face. I'm fully aware that describing a woman solely by her attributes is offensive, but Elena was the one girl I never got to know and I was so attracted to her that my memory was blunted. My instinct was to be polite and look away but I quickly learned that what's polite in a strip club is counter-intuitive: you must look *into* the boobs rather than away from them.

In my teens and early twenties I frequently had the sense that a madwoman was driving the car of my life while I sat in the back seat observing it and wondering how we ended up here. This was one of those moments.

That feeling ramped up to a new level seconds after Elena finished showing me how to dance, when I realized I was going to have to dance for Jim. My mind was numb with panic. I had no natural dancing abilities whatsoever and struggled to walk down the street without tripping over my own feet. Jim sat down and smiled up at me beatifically like a proud father at his daughter's nativity. Massive Attack's 'Unfinished Sympathy' started to play. This helped to a degree as I liked Massive Attack and couldn't have coped if it was some hair-rock stripper music like Mötley Crüe. Robotically, I copied Elena move for move, the robot shaking violently with nerves the whole time. I'm pretty sure I just took my bra off. I have no recollection of whether I took off all my street clothes during the lap dance – a ludicrous possibility, given it was 2007 and skinny jeans were at the height of their popularity. Maybe I started off in my underwear, which would have made way more sense but would have also been terrifying as a first-timer. Either way I fell forward stiffly and slid down Jim like a big lump with all the charisma of a shopfront mannequin before sliding back up and gawkily parroting, 'Thank you for a lovely dance.'

Jim beamed even more, the way you might smile at a Labrador that's learned how to high five.

'That was really your first time?'

I swelled with pride, wanting to believe his lie. He took me to the shift book to sign me up. A big blonde girl was in charge of it.

'Amber, can you sign up – what was your name going to be?'

'Uh, Ava,' I mumbled, cringing as soon as I'd said it. It didn't feel stripper-y enough. It felt pretentious. Already I felt like I'd be the misfit there. I like that I picked a palindrome – a word that's the same thing backwards and forwards. I remember seeing a Todd Solondz film called *Palindromes* about a girl called Aviva who could only ever be herself. That was my recurring problem in stripping: I couldn't be anyone but myself.

Amber was the head dancer and in simple terms she was blonde with big boobs and seemed like the stereotypical stripper but also had a wholesomeness and a jobsworth air about her that suggested she'd be just as at home managing a team of recruitment consultants.

'You should get your nails done,' she said, looking at my stubby hands. 'Only go to the Asians, though; they're the best.'

I balked at what I thought was mild racism, something that now seems ludicrous in the grand scheme of Things That Strippers Have Said to Me.

'Also, you can't wear those shoes.' I looked down at my black New Look heels I'd bought for a tenner. They were the only heels I owned as I'm 5 foot 10 and walking is enough of a challenge without adding a new difficulty setting. 'Simon the Shoe Guy will sell you shoes and you can either pay for them upfront or we take it out your earnings. He sells outfits as well. Lovely guy.'

Simon the Shoe Guy was not a lovely guy. Simon *was* that guy with a greasy ponytail in a leather jacket who, if you were casting for 'Grubby strip-club perverts', would be a shoo-in. Simon looked like he secreted oil rather than sweat. Simon would go round all the strip clubs in Edinburgh – maybe even all the strip clubs in Scotland, who knows – with one of those sports holdalls, filled to overflowing with Perspex heels, stockings and costumes.

He brought out a laminated brochure showing me near-identical stacked Perspex heels. They came in 6 or 10 inches. Some of them had a little secret slot in the platform where you could store your money and display how much money you were making. Bad if you've only made a fiver.

Simon did a sales pitch to me that seemed pointless given it was compulsory to wear this type of shoe. 'These lengthen the leg, lift the bum – the material is lightweight and excellent for gripping the pole.'

'I'll take the smallest heels,' I said. I remember they cost a lot for shoes that I definitely could never wear anywhere other than to this place without seeming mental.

Mel was the first girl I talked to on my first shift. As with any weird new environment I've been in where I felt shy – a psych hospital, a comedy club, a part-time job – no matter how unlikely it is that a person would be your friend in the outside world, you'll be their friend because they were nice to you on your first day.

Mel was from the outskirts of Edinburgh and was the same age as me but tiny and old-looking. She had no school qualifications and lived with her boyfriend and I'd never felt more middle class than when I was around her. I told her the saga of how the Scottish student funding body wouldn't listen to me about how skint I was and how I kept having to eke out a living from university hardship grants and how my dad earned a lot but wouldn't give me a penny. She nodded along to all this. I asked her why she was working there.

'I'm paying off my dad's funeral,' she said simply.

Her pole song was 'Dirty Diana', which I was embarrassed about for her but she was better than me and I needed a teacher. Your pole teacher in a strip club is whichever girl likes you enough to bother teaching you. She taught me pole from scratch, which I learned informally in 10-, 15- or 20-minute increments while we waited for customers to come in. The girls who worked full time were good at pole because they had to do a lot of waiting.

During my first proper lap dance after the club interview, I shook violently with nerves. This seemed odd to me down the line when it became as mundane as scanning shopping through a checkout.

In time it became the same reassuring routine: rub leg up man's leg; sway from side to side; rub opposite leg up man's leg; lean in close enough that they think you'll kiss them; pull away before they try anything; take bra off; lick right tit not left (left one inexplicably inflexible); slide down man onto floor; writhe around on floor; think what pasta to get from the Italian place at the end of my shift; the End.

Towards the end, you were meant to act as if you hoped this lap dance would never finish and then lean in and whisper, 'Would you like another dance?'

There were tiny variations you introduced to your routine as you learned more – like if the guy was smelly you'd do a lot less lap dancing and a lot more writhing around on the floor.

I think I got two dances on my first night. I feel like I'm supposed to say something wistful about how I remember their faces and who they were, but that's being overly generous to men and any meaning projected onto the job itself. The main thing I remember is how many men, in the absence of any touching, licked the air during lap dances. I also remember going for a smoke out the back on the fire escape on my first night and telling my friend Kev over the phone how groomed everyone was. He told me, 'I shared a taxi with some strippers once. They smelled like vanilla. It was *lovely*.'

I bought vanilla perfume from the Body Shop after that.

I immediately felt comfortable around my new colleagues. They were all so easy to talk to in comparison to the people at university who grimaced as soon as they heard my accent.

On my second night I talked to a chirpy girl who didn't seem very stripper-y at all.

'So how did you get into this?' she asked.

'I had a bad breakup,' I said, squishing the last two years down into something relatable.

Her, still chirpy: 'Oh my god, me tooooo! I had a breakup that was *so* bad and after that I was just like, *fuck it*.'

This wasn't uncommon, I found out later. Those of us that weren't 'stripper-strippers' just got into it one day as we were generally impulsive.

Big Daddy O's was a nice starter club but I'd heard there was more money elsewhere and it bugged me that every dance we did had 30 per cent taken off of us. Girls debated back and forth on the merits of this system versus paying a one-off house fee. On the one hand, the club taking a cut from every dance meant you could at least always make money on a quiet night and not leave in debt. But what was the point in playing it safe when you could pay a 50- or 70- quid house fee and keep everything you made after that? So, I moved from Big Daddy O's to Liquorice Club.

Liquorice Club felt like a grown-up strip club. Not always in a good way. The manager was an ex-stripper called Vicky and the assistant manager was a gay guy called Tom who would sometimes pole dance for us as a special treat – which was weird as he was chubby and grey-skinned and dressed like a Jobcentre advisor. I hated Vicky. She was blonde and bloated from champagne and boob jobs. Sometimes on really busy nights Vicky would strip too and it honestly felt like watching your mum dance drunk at your eighteenth as her hellish triple-G tits swung about the pole. I mean, *my* mum never did that but at the time the horror of seeing any woman over the age of 30 get up on stage was powerful.

Jordan was one of the head dancers. Jordan looked exactly like Marilyn Manson if he'd had a platinum wig and a Scottish accent. She wore black eyeshadow and dressed to match her hair – all in white with thigh-high PVC boots. She had been doing it for at least 10 years, an amount of time that to me at 20 seemed incomprehensible. She was the dictionary definition of a stripper so I was stunned to find out one night that she was a stone-butch lesbian with a long-term partner and often wished she could shave her head.

The other head dancer and Jordan's frequent work partner was Savannah. Savannah had the same standard-issue platinum-blonde hair as Jordan but with enormous tits and a kinder, almost kittenish face. A guy paid her to spit on him once, which I was always impressed with. I remember so clearly what a lot of them danced to. Jordan's song was always Marilyn Manson's cover of 'Tainted Love'. Savannah's was '#1 Crush' by Garbage, which opens with porn-y groaning, something I felt was a bit on the nose. I saw an interview with Shirley Manson and they asked if she knew her voice was the soundtrack of strippers everywhere. She said she did and she loved it, which made me like her more.

My song in Liquorice was 'Wide Open Space' by Mansun but this lent itself to stupid amounts of innuendo by bitchface Vicky every time she announced me: 'Good evening, guys. Next up on the pole showing you her *wide open space*, it's the lovely . . . Ava!'

I'd be standing onstage while she said this, nodding and smiling and weakly playing along with her dumb fanny jokes. I changed my song to 'Glory Box' by Portishead, which really wasn't much better in terms of innuendo as Vicky just started saying I was showing my glory box instead.

Innuendo has always annoyed me as a particularly English attempt at humour. It's saying but not quite saying something rude. In a Scottish strip club with bald fannies being waved about like Saltire flags at a gala day it felt ludicrous.

I stayed because the money was good. Until it wasn't and

Vicky started stealing off us. The general vibe of Liquorice Club girls was mean and hard-faced and although I got on okay there, I always felt like the dorky little sister who only narrowly escaped bullying. A lot of the women there had other jobs that involved some variation of being decorative ornaments to men. They would do car shows, which presumably involved draping yourself over a car in more or less the same costumes we wore to work.

Occasionally I'd try to leave but other jobs were so stiflingly boring and offensively underpaid that I'd always come back. Vicky would be sitting on the couches in the middle of the other girls, crowing triumphantly, 'She couldn't stay away!' as I walked past her, smiling tightly, into the changing rooms to put my Perspex shoes back on.

I couldn't find another job where I didn't get the sack when I was rude to the customers. Further, there was no other role that'd allow me to drag a guy on stage, tie a belt around his neck and make him bark like a dog while I kicked and throttled him. I couldn't find work anywhere else that involved watching a guy go from telling you he was a sommelier at one of Edinburgh's top restaurants to being dragged out by our skinhead bouncer while screaming, 'I just want beautiful women to piss on my face – what's so wrong about that? Huh?' It was always the most middle-class people who said the most disturbing things, likely because their ideas on working-class women's perceived coarseness meant they felt they could get away with it.

One stuffy English guy told me, 'I couldn't possibly get a dance; you look too much like my daughter.' Within half an hour he'd paid me to go into the dance room with him. An

Edinburgh University professor who insisted, 'No, no, no, you're too middle class to be doing this; I couldn't possibly . . .' quickly handed over his wallet with no hard sell on my part. My favourite customers were the Irish farmers who came over for a conference every summer. They were impeccably well behaved and seemed happy to just see a woman, any woman. One day I made £300 off one who was so drunk he fell asleep before even getting a dance. I woke him up every three minutes and took his money out his wallet while I stood over him fully clothed and watched as he nodded off again. I find a lot of TV shows overly humanize the men who use sex workers; like, they always try and have at least one scene that shows a gentle, human side to the whole thing, where a disabled man comes in or a man's wife has died or they just want a nice chat or some shit. I can't stress enough how far that was from my reality. I think those scenes are put in to appeal to men's egos because I never felt anything approaching sympathy for a single one of them. If there hadn't been security cameras I would have stolen their wallets.

There were levels of scary in strippers. Alanna was an entry-level bam. Lisa was Top Tier Mental. Lisa worked in my first club, Big Daddy O's, and made me feel as genteel as a kid from an Enid Blyton novel. On my first night, when I was tentatively voicing my concerns about having massive acrylic nails that stopped me doing basic tasks, she growled, 'Everything about you is gonna change in here. Yer hair, yer makeup. Everything!' and cackled dementedly. A couple of nights later, a man came in looking for Lisa. When she emerged from the back room, they shouted at each other and swore in what seemed to be delight, hugging and pulling back and shouting then hugging some more. I figured it was her regular and was jealous as I still didn't have one. She pulled back again, turning to face us: 'Everyone, this is my da! He just got out the jail!'

More and more of my friends were strippers and any attempt to even talk to university people outside of basic small talk felt pointless and unrewarding. Lauren did come to visit me one night with a couple of our gay mates but was put off after a stripper called Annie repeatedly accosted them, growling in a thick Romanian accent, 'You want dance?' every five minutes.

You needed at least one good friend so you had someone to rub fake tan on your back and do fake lesbian shows with. These consisted of kissing in front of a stag party before badly pretending to go down on each other by doing a bobbing head movement somewhere near your dance partner's inner thighs. It was a seriously bad sign of your status in the club if no one would do these things with you. Like smelly weird Alice, who'd licked someone's fanny *for real*. I felt bad for Alice; no one talked to her except me and she always had a telltale white patch in the centre of her back that was the hallmark of a girl without a single ally to rub in her fake tan. She invited me to go to a climbing wall with her but I knew from school that talking to unpopular girls would make things ten times worse for me so I declined.

We had a cast of regulars. First there was Mark. Mark was like part of the furniture, if you'd ever wanted to kick furniture. He was in his forties, bald with glasses and a completely blank look after a brain injury had knocked him out of his old office job. Mark's concrete rule – and a bizarre rite of passage for every new girl – was to get a dance with you on your first night and never again. Most people's first week at their new jobs involved them being taken to the local Wetherspoons or All Bar One to welcome them into the team; for us it was dancing for a guy with a brain injury.

Then there was Gary. Gary had Down's syndrome and was so small and stout as to appear completely spherical. He never got dances, just walked laps of the club bellowing the same two questions over the pounding R&B: 'Are ye having a good time? Are ye going out tonight?'

A chorus of polite: 'Aye, Gary, it's great, thanks. How are you?'

If you ignored him by going to practise on the pole, he'd walk up to the stage undeterred.

'Are ye having a good time?'

'No, Gary, I've brought shame on my parents and I'm living a double life.'

'Are ye going out tonight?'

As far as I knew, Gary never got a dance. Then a couple of years ago I met a Glasgow girl who said she'd tried a shift in that club. On her first night Gary had asked her for a dance then paid her by thrusting half a melted Twix into her hand. She shook her head in disbelief recounting the story.

'I never danced in Edinburgh after that.'

I've still to see a realistic portrayal of a strip club on TV. For me, it was a disco ball illuminating an empty room with a handful of girls sitting watching telly in PVC nurse costumes while two disabled men walked around shouting greetings at them.

*

We were always moving clubs or planning to move, chasing the money. My diary from 2008, scrawled in between reminders to finish the Classics gobbet on *Antigone*, notes my plans to go strip in Canada, which is oddly ambitious given I didn't know how to take the train to England at that point. We'd planned to strip in Iceland too but I bailed last minute. The two girls who went without me came back silent and looking miserable. It hadn't gone as hoped.

Often you'd go full circle and end up back where you started. After working at four different clubs I found myself back in Big Daddy O's. Post-recession, Jim had renamed it the Sapphire Rooms and had hung lots of blue velvet drapes in a bid to make it classy. In Dougie's absence some of Jim's hiring practices were questionable. He hired two dopey sisters from the Borders, Isla and Mhairi. Mhairi had bouncy brown curls, Isla bouncy blonde curls. Where Mhairi was stupid, Isla was daft in a way that you had to see to believe. They'd decided to become strippers after taking a pole fitness class, which is the equivalent to becoming a sniper in the army because you played *Call of Duty* once. None of us liked them. They were weirdly wholesome, stuck-up and continually breaking the rules with zero punishments. Isla had been caught kissing a customer in her first week. It was a great summer not in spite of but because of them. All of us united in our dislike of them.

Jim had brought in a bunch of dumb rules to try and improve the club's fortunes but anyone could see we weren't recession-proof; no one wanted lap dances, especially not from us. Jade had come back to work 5 stone heavier after having a baby and was crying in the dressing rooms in between shitting bright-orange oil from the diet meds she was taking. Some girls had to leave arm stockings or long gloves on during dances to hide their self-harm wounds.

One of the new rules was that you couldn't approach a customer as soon as he came in; you had to wait for him to go to the bar, order his drink in peace and sit down before you badgered him for a dance.

We all shook our heads in disgust as Isla immediately walked over to an old man that came in. We were annoyed but in that delicious collective way you experience as a group of women, which I hadn't felt before. Usually *I* was Isla, trampling blindly on social rules. Finally, I knew how good it felt; no wonder other women loved to gang up on me! This was power! This was unity! Four pairs of eyes burned a hole in Isla's back as she guided the old man to the sofas and sat opposite us, chatting away to him with a shamelessness that was breathtaking. We glowered and shook our heads some more while Isla remained totally oblivious. Increasing the volume, we muttered under our breath about how some people thought they were above the rules before Isla came bouncing over to our sofa, grinning.

'Guys, I'd like you to meet my dad.'

'Uh, are you joking?' I said.

To paint a fuller picture here, Isla was wearing a basque and a thong with her bare arse out, which was now facing her beaming elderly father as she spoke to us.

'Oh, I know,' she said, glancing behind her before lowering her voice as she leaned towards us. 'He's a bit embarrassing. D'you know, as soon as he got here he told me, "There are so many lovely ladies in here."'

I was starting to lose my grip on what was normal and whether I was the weird one for not having my dad come visit me. When we retold the story in every other dead shift that summer, Layla would repeat over and over that that was the moment I deadpanned, 'Yeah, *that's* what's embarrassing about this scenario.'

Not long after that, their younger brother started working behind the bar. The sisters would do lesbian pole shows on stage, grinding against each other while he smiled up at them like a cherub in a church fresco, pulling pints like it was all the loveliest thing in the world. Maybe we were secretly jealous of them. Most of us couldn't tell our families on pain of death so to see a whole family acting like it was normal was hard.

In 2020 the British documentary-maker Louis Theroux made a programme on sex work* that – unlike the majority of his output – was met with some negativity after viewers and media alike believed it exploited the sex workers it featured. One of the most aggrieved interviewees was an autistic woman whose autism was referred to once in the programme and never again, despite her visibly stimming, rubbing her hands together and fidgeting anxiously while speaking to Louis. As with the vast majority of documentaries on sex work, the show seemed to exist mainly to gawp at misfit women. Louis's trademark

---

* *Louis Theroux: Selling Sex* (2020).

voiceover ponderously wonders why someone would do this job, ignores her autism, fails to draw any real conclusions, goes back to asking why on earth anyone would do the job and then brings the programme to a close, while the viewer learns absolutely nothing new.

And yet, to anyone versed in how female autism presents, the autistic interviewee's story shines through regardless. At one point she tells her confused-looking interviewer: 'No one wants to be around me for who I am. People want to be around me for what I can give to them. And, like, for most men what I can give to them is sex.'

Theroux had made an earlier documentary on autistics* but it only covered those with high support needs and viewers were shown images more commonly associated with the condition: mostly male kids being sat on during violent meltdowns, speaking very little or not at all, their parents crying with frustration. The vast majority of people's understanding of autism is sparse and informed by people who are autism-adjacent rather than the autistics themselves, so it's infuriating that when we do finally identify ourselves to the media we're so easily dismissed. Instead, the programme-makers lazily pedalled the same old substandard narrative of 'sex worker with low self-esteem'. The idea of the autistic sex worker is so much more interesting and explains the motivations so much more clearly.

---

* *Louis Theroux: Extreme Love – Autism* (2012).

Chapter Nine

'And I was fat then . . . You can be fat and strip. I didn't have a gimmick. I see girls now who are trying to be alternative. They won't make a dime. You've got to have white pumps, pink bikini, fuckin' hairpiece, pink lipstick. Gold and tan and white. If you even try and slip a little of yourself in there you won't make any money.'

—Courtney Love

Stripping was becoming draining. It wasn't the bare boobs of it all; in fact, I spent an inordinate and ultimately dispiriting amount of my shifts trying to persuade people to look at them. Rather, it was the small talk I had to have while freezing in my underwear, the endless procession of timewasters, the bloodsucking emotional labour. I was back at the Liquorice Club, reading 'Prufrock' on shift, trying to keep up with my coursework in the early-evening lull, convinced that when T S

Eliot wrote, 'And I have known the eyes already, known them all—/ The eyes that fix you in a formulated phrase,' he meant seeing Mark and Gary and the man in the stupid white linen suit for the third time in a row that week.

I couldn't keep having the same conversation every night. I couldn't work out the perfect thing to say to get customers' money. Worse, I couldn't complain to anyone on the outside as I knew they'd say: 'Of course stripping is awful – what did you think it'd be?'

I couldn't handle the guilt of my double life either. I was having a recurring nightmare where I was on the pole and as I took my bra off triumphantly, the lights would come up and I'd realize with horror that the strip club had turned into my local church and the priest and Mum and Dad and Jesus-on-the-cross were all there.

It makes sense, though, for an autistic woman to be good at the job, because you're essentially masking using a well-known female stereotype and the persona you have to adopt while stripping seemed no less ridiculous to me than any of the others I'd been expected to put on my whole life.

It was 2008 and Britain was in a recession so the men who came in just wanted to watch some pole dancing for free then waste our time with chit-chat before telling us they weren't the type of guy to go to a strip club, which is what 100 per cent of men in strip clubs say. After two years in those places, I still didn't know who to be to them or who they wanted me to be. Still, without question the worst of times were when I was completely myself with them.

One time I got talking to a preppy-looking boy my age on

a quiet weeknight when it emerged that we were at the same university.

'I'm a student there too!' I shouted over the music, tugging my negligee down, suddenly self-conscious.

'No way,' he laughed. 'Which course?'

'English lit.'

'Me too!'

We chatted for a bit about what modules we'd both taken and some of the lecturers we had in common. As I stood up to find paying customers I said to him earnestly, 'Well, I hope you take from this we're not just a bunch of stereotypes; a lot of us are just regular students.' He nodded thoughtfully. I beamed at him and headed off.

A few weeks later my boyfriend told me about the creative-writing class he'd just had where one of the guys read out a story he had written about a stripper. He showed it to me, reading out the dumbest parts. There were a lot of clumsy descriptions of her thick red lips and coarse blonde hair and how she'd wept as her drunk husband punched her to the ground. The story ended with her sobbing on the kitchen floor, enormous breasts heaving as she took another swig of whisky from the bottle.

'So, uh . . . he said it was based on a stripper he chatted to when he went to the Liquorice Club.' He laughed, looking up at me from the page. He didn't love that I did the job but quietly tolerated it in the absence of an alternative source of cash.

'Rugby shirt? Preppy-looking?'

'Yeah.'

'Right, yeah, met him.' I nodded grimly.

It was good to know that while I was agonizing over the right thing to say to customers, they were taking in precisely none of what I said anyway. I'd come to understand that the guys who said they wanted to get to know the real me in the strip club were the personality equivalent of men who said, 'You look better without makeup.' It doesn't mean anything; they just say it 'cause it sounds good. But the idea that no makeup equals natural beauty is strikingly similar to the notion that inside every stripper there is a 'real' version of that person, a sweet, kind, simple girl. The fact that this in itself was a secondary layer of protection we adopted to safeguard ourselves from these men and their violence entirely escaped them.

Selling lap dances is essentially the same as being a cold-calling salesman with the added indignity that you're in your pants while you're trying to negotiate the deal. To keep our enthusiasm up, each of us would start the night with a target in our heads for what we wanted to make by the end of the shift. Pulling their heels on backstage, the air in the changing rooms heady with Femfresh, most girls would mutter to themselves, '£500 tonight. Definitely . . .' while I, recognizing my limits and low tolerance for 80 per cent of the customers, would think, *Maybe £100?*

After 17 gruelling rounds of 'I don't really want a dance', 'I'm just here for a quiet drink' and 'Maybe later', I'd finally made my target one night and was queuing up to pay our house fees when Vicky, the boss, overcharged us for commission. This meant I instantly lost the money I'd made that evening and was going home with . . . Well, definitely not enough to justify doing *this*. If your family are gonna disown you over your job, you want to be making the kind of cash that makes you indifferent to what they think. But the club was losing money hand over fist and they were using us dancers to absorb the loss. It was the final straw. I looked around, waiting for the other girls to kick off. There was some quiet chatter in the changing rooms of moving to a rival club but no one wanted to stand up to Vicky – not after she'd had her dogs chase another stripper down the stairs earlier in the week.

'But that's . . . But commission is always 70 on a Saturday!'

She looked at me blankly. 'If you don't like it, go work another club.'

I glanced at the caged Alsatians under her desk and turned round, walking down the stairs, clenching my fists in impotent fury.

I walked home with Sara, ranting all the way through the Meadows about the commission and what a scam it was and why we should unionize. We reached the park near my flat when she spun around to face me, her accent ramping up a notch in anger, going more Northern as her face flushed red.

'Can you fookin' stop? Have you heard yourself? 'Cause I can't listen to it anymore.'

I was stunned.

She carried on: 'This job is my one bit of relief from my maths course and you bitch and complain and bitch and complain. Here's a thought: don't do it if you don't like it.'

Mortified, I wondered how long she'd been annoyed by me. I'd always just assumed we had a shared hatred of the place. I couldn't wrap my head round how anyone could be stripping to relax.

*

A few days later, my phone rang when I was getting ready for an afternoon shift. It was my dad.

'Papa's had a stroke. He's not likely to make it.'

I started crying, told him I'd get myself to the hospital then hung up the phone and continued to cry the whole time I was in the shower.

'Waaaaaah,' I cried as I dried my hair. I got dressed, packed my bag and got the train home.

Papa was my maternal grandfather, the normal, non-drunk one. A coal miner turned music teacher, he delighted in presenting me increasingly impossible books of Chopin nocturnes to play on the piano. I'd chat to him on the phone daily, much more often than I spoke with anyone else in my family.

I went to see him in the hospital every day. The way Catholics deal with dying is remarkably similar to the way they deal with sex in that they seem to find both things very embarrassing and prefer not to acknowledge their existence. Since euthanasia is illegal in Britain, when someone has a stroke and isn't going to survive, the doctors starve and dehydrate them to death.[*]

Despite this, everyone crammed into the little intensive-care room kept trying to make out that Papa was having the time of his life. As we pulled up chairs around his bed, some gasbag great-aunt insisted over and over that this death was way better than any of the other deaths she'd seen in the family.

---

[*] I'm aware that this process was called the Liverpool Care Pathway by the NHS but for reasons outlined elsewhere in this book, I don't do well with obfuscating language. I think if we all called it 'starving and dehydrating someone to death' a lot more of us would become pro-euthanasia overnight.

The only thing we were told we could do to alleviate Papa's discomfort of being starved and dehydrated to death was to dip cotton buds in a glass of water and drip them into his parched open mouth. Thick yellow gunk was crusted around his lips and I thought how this was objectively something that would normally turn my stomach. Now, though, I dropped the water into his mouth, stroked his head and whispered to him, hoping his coma dreams weren't too hellish. People at weddings and on Instagram go on about love in this saccharine way. I realized then that actually, love is dropping water into someone's gross deathbed mouth.

'Sorry, I'm not a great nurse,' I told him, still there at midnight, wiping away mouth-goo.

'Good nurse,' he mumbled back, eyes still closed.

This incident would quickly be refashioned by my family as something I'd imagined to comfort myself, even though they were the ones insisting this coma was the best he'd ever looked.

After a week of spending every day by his bed, we all went home and I took a sleeping tablet to try and switch off. We were then all woken up in the early hours by a call from the hospital telling us that he was dying or whatever redundant euphemism they used. We got to his room just as he was doing these crazy breaths.

'Is that a death rattle?' I slurred. The sleeping pill hadn't worn off and as a result I was more autistic than usual and needed the facts clearly laid out in front of me.

'He's at peace now,' the nurse corrected me.

'Ugghhh,' Papa's corpse croaked.

I pointed at him and repeated my question: 'But is that a death rattle?'

'It's okay,' said the nurse in a soothing voice that made me want to throttle her.

I wasn't sure what it would take for this bitch to admit the guy was dead. It was fairly self-evident that the worst thing had happened so everyone's efforts to try and smooth it over were hilarious to me. I was once at a wake in Donegal where the dearly departed had died by falling off a cliff and breaking his neck. Rigor mortis had set in at an awkward angle so instead of lying in peaceful repose, the guy's head was at a 45-degree angle as if he was checking out who'd turned up to see him. 'Ah, sure, he looks lovely,' I caught someone saying to his purple dead body in the coffin.

I felt like I'd lost the only friend I had in the family. When I went back to work a fortnight later, everyone complimented me on being thinner. I knew I needed to take advantage of my temporarily flat stomach to turn a profit but I found it hard to grieve and simultaneously be sexy on the pole. My parents' belief that my dead relatives could see everything I was doing from heaven was niggling me. *Well, at least from heaven you can see how little money I have,* I reasoned with Papa's ghost, figuring that in the afterlife he'd be blessed with an angelic, non-judgemental attitude and would just be smiling down on me benevolently.

A month after my return, I had a total mental collapse in the club after dragging myself in for a Friday shift. There's no HR in strip clubs so you can be mentally ill for a long time before it becomes a problem and whether it'll ever even become a problem really depends on what flavour of madness you've got. A manic upswing and you've got yourself a girl who'll do anything in a £20 dance. Crippling depression that freezes you to your seat is less ideal. That was what kicked in for me that night. Hunched over in my bikini, my bare arse rooted to the cold leather couches, unable to pump myself up to approach the fresh batch of wankers that had arrived. Luckily, they came over and started talking to me instead.

One of them nudged the other before he spoke: 'Can I ask you something? Are you horny on your period?'

The man snorted with laughter, turned to his friends and they fell about in hysterics. It's important you know what they looked like so you don't write them off as Bad Men, other men, not like the men *you* know. They were middle-class professionals with the anglicized accents that marked them out as Edinburgh private-school boys. These were the kind who'd never had to wait a table, never mind smile and nod and dance and smile and be sweet and obliging to people who would spit on you given half the chance.

One of the group objected mildly to him saying this.

'What? I'm asking her!'

More laughter.

I got up and walked away, saying nothing. A distorted, very high-pitched *wheeeeee* noise filled my head. More men came over and asked for dances. 'Go away,' I told them. 'Fuck off.'

From here on in, my memories become nightmarish little shards. I remember attending a student newspaper social and having to stand up and give a speech for the reviews page I edited. All I could hear the entire time I was speaking was the same high-pitched sound playing over everything. The only way I gauged that what I was saying was weird was by clocking the looks of concern and embarrassment on others' faces. I couldn't feel my arms or torso or legs. I remember observing the scene from the ceiling and thinking: *Oh no, I've gone mad again.*

This was followed by a ridiculous self-harming session back at my flat with – of all things – a blunt serrated breadknife. As I sawed at my arm like it was a stale loaf, I reflected on how self-harming was already so embarrassing that if you were gonna do it you should at least have the right tools and I wasn't even capable of that. I was terrified of going to sleep so decided it was best to avoid it. After multiple nights of having no idea if I'd slept or not, I stood outside the university GP practice at 6am, waiting for them to open, my breath visible in the freezing cold.

Talking to them with the white noise still in my head, only hearing fragments of what I said over the din, I registered myself saying: 'I can't . . .'

From underwater I heard the doctor tell me that 'This is just a granny dose' of something called zopiclone, a hypnotic that would bring a bad taste to my mouth before sucking me under – but only enough to make me feel groggy when what I wanted was to be knocked out for days, weeks even. The university signed me off sick but I have no recollection of how that happened, only that from this point on I didn't leave my flat for a couple of months.

My mum and teen brother came through to Edinburgh and took me out for Japanese food as there was no other way in our culture of saying, 'Sorry you've gone mad again.' I told them I'd realized it was my life's purpose to become a stand-up comedian. Their faces wrinkled with concern at how unwell I was.

'But you're always saying I'm funny?' I offered.

They shifted in their seats and exchanged glances. 'Yes, but . . .' And silence. No one followed up the 'but' or explained why I shouldn't do it.

Nowadays I think of this breakdown as more of an autistic shutdown. Faced with the pretty daunting task of working a full-time night job alongside a full-time degree course teamed with extracurricular writing for the newspaper to ensure I became a big deal and never had to go back to Bathgate, something was bound to snap. Having exhausted all other options, my brain turned on the white noise to force me to have a break.

Chapter Ten

Back at work and unwilling to spend one more second of my leisure time engaged in small talk with men, I started dating women more and wondered whether maybe the weird alien feeling I had all the time was because I was gay. This was an appealing answer, a neat one illustrated by all the gay TV and film I was watching. I'd seen how this story played out: there would be difficulties along the way but I'd be helped by my many gay friends and in the end find resolution in the form of a clear sexual identity. It didn't work out this way. If anything, women's social codes were ten times less readable than men's and they seemed to need a lot more emotional support than I could ever give them. Beyond a first date, I had no idea what to say to them; and even though I liked having sex with them, I didn't fit in on the gay scene either, where everyone seemed to already be friends and I felt like I'd missed out on some big initial meeting.

One date asked me when I'd first come out to my parents

and I panicked that if I told the truth I'd have failed some gay authenticity test. This feeling is recurrent in autistics.[*] If you've ever started school midway through the school year or been the new person at work and felt lost – it's that feeling. Except you never just pick up on stuff or fall in line eventually; it's a constant sense that everyone is in a WhatsApp group you don't know about.

The girl was still waiting for me to reply. I was concentrating hard on lying.

'You have come out to your parents, right?'

'Oh, ages ago,' I lied. 'They're really cool with that kind of thing,' I said, thinking of Mum telling me I was only doing it to show off and of Natalie and the necklace. I then worried that my lying meant I was a fraud, so to redeem myself I had sex with her and came and wondered whether the fact that she was butch meant I was properly gay and why nothing I did helped me to fit in anywhere.

In autumn I was dating a nice girl student and left her for a nice boy student. They may as well have been the same person, they were such wholesome middle-class Scots. The resentment I felt towards these people made it hard to find a connection. They had their weekends free, they got free money from their parents and there was an innocence to them and a carefree air that meant they might as well have been ten years younger than me.

---

[*] Many autistics are queer in some way or have a non-traditional sexual identity.

My envy of them was such that I could taste the bile whenever I spoke to them. I hated how weird I felt around them and how I now saw myself.

I went to live with Lauren. I was working at the Burke & Hare and being bullied by some of the other girls there. They were a group of pneumatic-titted blondes who were a far cry from the amiable group of weirdos at the Sapphire Rooms. I was so, so tired. Trying to dance at nights, writing for the paper and reading the insane amount for the third-year coursework was knackering.

I remembered what Jeanette Winterson said that day at the Book Festival: *'You just had to work bloody hard.'*

I am *working hard,* I thought. I groaned in frustration then promptly fell asleep face-down in my books.

Everyone was suddenly being nice to me at the newspaper. I'd been nominated for a *Guardian* award for writing funny little columns. Having had enough of the Burke & Hare bullies, I was now back at the Sapphire Rooms. I ran in, waving the newspaper at the dancers. They gathered round and studied it, proud of me.

'This is me,' I said to one of the customers, pointing to my photo in the paper. 'I'm a writer outside of here.'

'I don't really want a dance,' he said.

It was my final year of university and things weren't going great with my latest boyfriend, Josh. We were walking home from a night out when he said, 'You really love to tell the same stories over and over again.'

This was true. I also used the exact same phrases and level of enthusiasm every time, pitching my voice the same, rising and falling at the same points. He seemed put out by it but it's something that later became useful when I had to do it for 50 dates in a row on stand-up tours. He was also freaked out by me after we were supposed to go to a cocktail bar on my birthday night out. It was a night out for the student newspaper too and everyone was celebrating us winning big at the awards. I'd patiently waited and waited and waited for us to go to this cocktail place, wondering if my boyfriend had forgotten we were going. I'd looked at my watch. It was getting late; we weren't going to make it. Eventually I'd exploded, freaking out at him: 'We're in the wrong bar! We're supposed to be at Dragonfly!'

He'd looked at me baffled. 'What the fuck? Why do you care? Everyone's having a nice time here.'

'Okay but we *have* to go to the other bar now.'

'Why?!'

I hadn't known what to tell him other than, 'Because you said we were going there.' I was an adult but the horror in not doing the scheduled activity was making me feel increasingly helpless. I could see the disgust and confusion in his face.

There's a stereotype about brides freaking out if their wedding day doesn't match the dream day they've imagined in their head. This is the closest I can get to explaining what most social plans and holidays are like for me. If a bride freaks out on her hen night or at her wedding, knowing looks will be exchanged because it's been shown over and over again in media and films that that's just what brides do. There's a level of understanding. There's no such thing for autistic women so instead we look mad or like we're being deliberately difficult.

Now I'm in a relationship where we both know I have autism, Conor understands my sheer panic at any kind of uncertainty so a night out will be scheduled a lot more like this: 'At this hour we will do *this*, then we will go *here*, then *here*.' Some degree of flexibility is built in too to allow for unforeseen changes.

'Okay, Fern, there are then two options: you can do *this* or *this*,' he'll say.

I go on holidays these days but my version of getting excited about them is researching the temperature of the sea, the distance from the hotel to a cafe, the distance from the hotel to a bar, planning what I will eat every day down to the tiniest details. I then try and imagine every bad thing that could possibly happen so I won't be surprised. I imagine small tragedies, like the meltdown I will have on Day 1 from the change of environment, to big ones, like Conor drowning in the sea and me flying home single.

During the summer holidays I had been reviewing comedians and interviewing playwrights for an arts magazine while stripping at night to pay for the privilege. My editor ordered me to try stand-up and write an article about it. I spent six weeks shaking and feeling nauseous but was secretly thrilled at the opportunity. He'd had no idea I wanted to do it anyway; but if he hadn't told me to I'd have kept sending secret letters to local comedy clubs asking for advice and hoping someone in my personal life would tell me I was good enough, so it never would have happened. This way I was forced to do it.

Before the gig, I lost my voice so it was a hoarse croak. I took myself off to the same campus GP who had seen me through every bout of going mad, who immediately said it was smoking and to quit. Case closed. Over the next ten years I went on to lose my voice once a year. I quit smoking, alcohol, being out in noisy bars. I drank lemon in warm water till I was sick of it. Nothing helped. When I got my diagnosis, I found out that I'd been getting so stressed I was tensing my whole body and my breathing was becoming shallow. I stopped losing my voice after that.

Throughout my first gig, my hand shook violently trying to hold the mic and my material was underwritten to the point of being non-existent; but the feeling of being on stage was both euphoric and weirdly normal. The occasional embarrassed laugh from a baffled audience was all the encouragement I needed to keep going.

Afterwards, I lay in bed next to my boyfriend, staring at the ceiling, wide-eyed and unable to sleep. I'd never had this feeling before about anything other than the early bit of falling in love. Previously, all that had mattered was boyfriends and books. Achieving academic stuff felt good but this was different. It was like Josh was now a ghost, an outline of a person next to me in bed, his significance gone. I knew with a horrible certainty that I was going to have to keep doing this forever. I wouldn't need to worry about anything again as I'd always have this thing I could do that made me feel amazing. This had to be what heroin felt like. I decided to keep the feeling to myself because it was so special and so life-changing that I had to protect it like a baby bird.

At breakfast I mentioned to Josh that I might like to do another gig.

'I don't think you should do it again.'

'Oh? Uh . . . Why?'

'You were so nervous and in such a state about it I don't know why you would do anything like that again. It made you so unhappy.'

His (male, privileged) friend agreed when I brought it up again later. 'Comedy is much harder than it looks.'

I fretted a little but opted not to take advice off someone who'd never done anything for himself in his life, never mind a gig.

I made *hmm* noises of agreement but retreated into my head and started planning. For the rest of my final year I researched gigs, comedy forums and the best places to live to do comedy in the UK. While Josh and I studied next to each other for our finals, I was furtively applying to do every single gig and stand-up competition I could find.

At the start of my final year in Edinburgh I was made editor of the university newspaper, which meant two things. I couldn't keep working full time in a strip club in addition to running a newspaper and doing my dissertation. And if I couldn't get the Scottish student funding body to acknowledge that I was financially independent from my parents I was going to have to leave and it'd all have been for nothing anyway. The stress was unsustainable. I stopped short of telling them I'd been funding myself through working every titty bar in Edinburgh but in a last-ditch attempt to convince them I'd gathered a dossier of evidence and got a letter from the university's student-hardship office confirming that I was a regular visitor and had been well known to them for a number of years (I'd once asked them straight-faced whether I could sell my blood or eggs in this country).

I headed out to the industrial estate where they were based. The man at the desk studied the evidence I'd handed over, then disappeared into a back office for a while. I felt despondent. None of my previous attempts had worked. I texted my co-editor that he'd likely need to find someone else. The man returned to his desk.

'Turns out we made a mistake. Let's get this sorted.'

Overnight I was given four years' worth of grants. I was stunned into silence. I could quit stripping. When I woke up after the best sleep of my life, I realized that those people who say money isn't everything are liars.

Chapter Eleven

Graduation time. I broke up with Josh.

I remember almost nothing about the guy's personality so I've no idea why I went insane with grief. I think now I was sad because there was too much change: university ending, the prospect of moving to England for my postgrad and a breakup. He could have been anyone and I'd have reacted the same.

I was still intermittently shagging him but crying afterwards every time. 'I'm sorry, I'm really not a crier . . .' I'd say, crying.

'You have this whole other idea of yourself. Like, you say you're not a crier but you're crying right now,' he'd reply.

I don't know if my alexithymia is solely linked to autism.[*] I do

---

[*] Alexithymia is the limited ability to recognize and describe the emotions you're feeling. It also means your mind fails to register the physical symptoms of anxiety as early as it should. People with alexithymia are not emotionless; rather, we feel huge emotions but there's a disconnect in our ability to properly acknowledge them.

know that in my teens and early twenties the flurry of stressful events – from being kicked out of home, to working in strip clubs at the same time as being at uni – all became so insanely painful that it reminded me of the time I had an exposed nerve after getting my wisdom tooth out. The pain would reach an absolute peak, to the point I felt I'd pass out. Then endorphins would rush in and make me feel I was in a trance. At some point with all the stress I think that was what happened.*

After quitting stripping and getting my student grant, I had a much more stereotypical student life. To distract me from the split from Josh, some poshos who were more his friends than mine invited me to Catherine and Edward something-or-other's parents' beach house. Even with my new bank balance I may as well have been a refugee in terms of how out of place I felt. I didn't fit in with the Edinburgh University girls, who were uniformly thin, had messy blonde hair and pearls, had travelled the world and said everything confidently even when they were staggeringly wrong.

We had a barbecue at the beach house and everyone started fondly reminiscing about some amazing place they all went to. I realized they were talking about their boarding school. Without a posh boyfriend there as a buffer I just could not navigate these people. I tried to work out how I could join in, my mind

---

* Autistic people are between 25 and 50 per cent more likely to have alexithymia than the general population is but alexithymia is also a coping mechanism from PTSD. In turn autistic people – due to various factors such as our low social status, our vulnerability to being rejected by family, mental illness, social isolation – are far more likely to be traumatized so it's tricky to separate one from the other.

scrambling for some vaguely positive memory of school to share alongside theirs. I gave it a go in my head: *Oh, that's like the time we all had to do trust exercises in the mental unit* . . .

I stayed silent and shovelled food into my mouth instead.

'Fern's enjoying the potato salad – maybe a little too much?' said a Catherine or a Chloe.

'Sorry, do you not want me to . . . Do you want some?' I thrust the bowl towards her.

She smiled nastily. 'No, you enjoy.'

There's a curious yet rarely discussed tendency among middle- and upper-class women to police what each other eat. I've only ever come across it among these groups. It seems to be passed down from mother to daughter and is the cause of so much stress. For all her flaws, my mum never raised me with dysfunctional attitudes to food or made me think I was greedy or not thin enough. She was always clear she disliked me for *me*.

The girls at the table talked with hushed reverence about Will's new girlfriend, an anxious, quiet girl who was emaciated and rumoured to be bulimic. She wasn't with us on this weekend but I'd been for dinner with them both the week before and she'd got up to rush to the toilets immediately after the meal.

'Is she away to make herself sick?' I'd asked through a mouthful of mashed potato.

'Yeah,' he'd said, looking wistfully at her as she rushed off before adding admiringly, 'but just look at those legs.'

Back at the beach house, we played a dreadful parlour game where you bounced up and down trying to grab an ever-diminishing muesli box with your teeth. I got stoned and couch-locked, watching the scene unfold in mute horror. A cheery, ruddy-cheeked girl who looked like she'd never had anything bad said to her did the splits and picked up the muesli box, flicking her hair back triumphantly and grinning as she stood back up.

'Rachel's getting a little *too* good at yoga!' someone said and everyone laughed like it was the funniest thing they'd ever heard.

I missed my stripper friends.

The next day I woke up in my twin bed to the sound of the other girls all shrieking delightedly.

'Julian and Edward are going birdwatching!'

They said it with the same excitement we'd felt the night a famous children's TV presenter hired out the VIP room at the strip club. At breakfast I dropped my sausages on the floor so that my only ally on the trip, a Labrador called Coco, could snaffle them.

It was a sunny Saturday morning when I got a phone call from Will to say that Josh was shagging Millie and that he'd wanted to tell me so I didn't get a nasty surprise later and would I like to go and watch a movie with them all at the cinema? I laughed as this was clearly one of Will's sick pranks. Will's voice stayed serious. I laughed again – 'Fuck off, Will' – and hung up. I stood and stared at my phone in my hand for a moment.

Millie.

Millie was a little po-faced blonde who wept at the end of every night out and held everyone up from going to watch the

Pixies at Primavera when she took an hour to eat a canapé-sized burger. *Millie*? I thought about how Josh and I had met in that working-class literature module. We used to laugh about how spoiled and privileged everyone at university was. They'd be the last two to get together. It wasn't even conceivable.

I phoned Josh just in case. I laughed as I started to speak 'cause it sounded so ridiculous coming out of my mouth. 'Will says you're fucking Millie.'

He didn't say anything.

Some of the pranks Will does, man, I thought to myself.

Josh cleared his throat. 'I thought it'd be best for you to find out rather than turning up at the cinema and—'

I hung up. I went cold all over and my stomach lurched.

Fuckin' *Millie.*

Not true, not true, not true.

At this point my flatmates arrived back at the flat with Lauren in tow. I turned to them and shouted, 'Josh's having sex with Millie!' before clutching my sides and folding in half as if I'd been punched in the stomach.

I managed to get up and run to the toilet and started to heave. The thought of someone I trusted – someone I *loved* – fucking a privately educated Tory was just too much to bear.

My flatmates sprang into action to comfort me. Lauren opened a bottle of Prosecco and rushed it towards me like a paramedic with IV fluids.

A couple of bottles later, we headed out to a bar. Emboldened by despair and grief, I went up to the best-looking guy there. 'Hold me,' I ordered.

His name was Steve. He worked in something boring like

insurance and was just the sort of vacuous, empty-headed everyman I needed in my life right then.

The day after I learned about Josh and Millie, I woke up with grotesque biblical sores forming all over my body. They were open and angry-looking. I went to the GP.

'Has anyone close to you died recently?' he asked.

'No but I had a bad breakup,' I said.

'Only because we usually see this in people suffering from extreme grief. Their immune systems can't cope.'

I tried to explain that it was utterly inconceivable to me that my boyfriend would fuck a privately educated blonde Tory but I felt like old male doctors didn't understand that stuff. It made perfect sense to me that my skin was bursting open in disgusting weeping pustules. The emotions felt volcanic and I'd never been good at communicating that to people in words so now my body was doing it for me.

I got back in touch with another guy called Steve, who I'd met on holiday but ghosted. Initially I saved him and the Steve from the bar in my phone as 'Steve 1' and 'Steve 2' respectively, but as the summer dragged on, I grimly decided to just label them both 'Steve' so I could play a sort of Steve Russian roulette and see which one showed up at my door when I texted either number.

I can't even remember what summer job I had as I stopped eating or sleeping again around then and got sacked from whatever it was.

I started working in the Citizens Advice Bureau on South Bridge and, after reading about a celebrity who lost a ton of weight from only eating eggs, I decided that I too would only eat eggs. As I had no appetite this was pretty easy. I could do maybe four to eight boiled eggs a day. It was incredibly comforting to reduce everything to one food.

I pounded the treadmill chanting, *Josh and Millie Josh and Millie Josh and Millie* . . . in my head. Any time I got tired, I'd picture him stroking her little ribs in bed and them laughing together about what a fat unsophisticated lump I was.

JOSHANDMILLIE!JOSHANDMILLIE! I'd scream in my head as I kept running. I'd cry in the toilet cubicles after and wonder what people were on about when they talked about endorphins from exercise making them happier.

The magazine I had worked for with Josh in the summer break were having a launch party. Knowing I would see him and her together as a couple at the event made it really real. I'd gone from a size 12 down to a size 8 which is no mean feat at 5 foot 10.

As Lauren and I walked over to the venue I had a joint while reassuring her: 'This way I'll be so relaxed. There's no way I'll try and fight her.'

But as soon as Millie walked in I realized that weed wasn't a miracle drug. She was in a black lace dress with big red lips, clinging on to Josh, her googly eyes bugging out when she spotted me in the crowd. I casually walked past and accidentally-on-purpose shoulder bumped her.

Josh came over immediately. 'You're not welcome here,' he said vehemently.

'*She*'s not welcome here!' I fired back, feeling I was playing a part badly in *EastEnders*.

'She's more welcome here than you are.'

I looked around for the first time at the crowd of freaked-out rich kids, the future power players in British media, and realized he was probably right.

The editors and people in charge of the party had already taken me outside for a quiet word and I'd promised them all that I'd be good. Their faces revealed that they'd never experienced this type of scenario before, since all parties at our university tended to be thematic and very carefully structured jolly fun. This was key to their downfall. They'd believed me and let me go back inside.

As soon as Millie went to the toilets alone, I followed her. I watched her entering a cubicle and I high-kicked the door in.

Kapow!

She clung to the cistern, looking frightened but with an infuriating half-smile on her face. She reminded me of a painting of a noblewoman or a Tudor queen.

'You . . .' I trailed off as I thought of my scholarship and post-university jobs and the fact that if I got in trouble ever again I'd only be ruining things for myself. '. . . *Bitch*,' I said weakly.

And with that, light-headed from the eggs and wobbly on my revenge heels, I walked out.

Back in the main room, Lizzie – one of the kinder posh girls – came up to me. 'Fern! You look amazing!' she said, in raptures while I finally achieved acceptance into the middle classes through thinness.

'Thanks. I haven't been eating,' I replied flatly, looking over her shoulder to continue glaring at Millie.

Lizzie's face crumpled with dismay. *Well, what the fuck did you want me to say?* I thought as she turned to chat to someone else. The noise and the lights and the odd pain in my stomach meant I couldn't do my Edinburgh University girl act anymore.

I had to find someone to have sex with that night. There was no other option. By this point, though, Steve 1 had broken it off with me after realizing I was only going to take him to the party as my revenge date and I'd decided I couldn't just have Steve 2 on my phone. I needed someone new in the rotation. A kind, soft-hearted leftie from Bristol who I'd been on one chaste date with kept bobbing about on the fringes of my conversations smiling at me. The idea of someone caring for me, who liked me for me, was revolting to me right then and the last thing I wanted. I ignored him and tried chatting up a disinterested-looking news reporter who worked with my flatmate. His indifference was extremely hot to me. Unfortunately, just as I got him to talk to me I realized I'd have to excuse myself as the gnawing pain in my stomach was driving me to distraction. That, and the joint I had on the way over was making it hard to speak coherently and follow the conversation.

I walked over to the dancefloor, where Lauren – an avowed homosexual – was passionately getting off with a guy (a future BBC correspondent, it turned out). I tugged at her sleeve. 'Hey – I think I'd like to leave now.' As if in slow motion, I watched Millie telling Josh, Josh telling security and security walking menacingly in my direction. Time sped up again and I made surprisingly quick calculations of how to react because I couldn't suffer the indignity of being dragged out in a strapless dress with one or both of my boobs making an unexpected guest appearance. 'I'll just get you outside,' I said hurriedly to

Lauren and then tried to style it out by walking out with security on either side of me.

A week later, a fat bearded geek, with one of those accents that tries desperately to distinguish its speaker from common Scottish plebs, harangued me at the table using my full name.

'Why are you doing this, Fern Brady?'

'Because I want to do comedy.'

'Yes, but why are *you* doing this?' he spluttered. 'I mean you're already good at other stuff. You do journalism, right? So why do this?'

This was my welcome to the intensely male Scottish comedy scene. I was the only woman sitting at the table at the open-mic night in Tollcross. The atmosphere was tense. When I walked on stage at these places they played stuff like 'All the Single Ladies' or introduced me mockingly as 'The beautiful Miss Fern Brady' and generally did as much as possible to put me at a disadvantage. Any illusion of women being supportive was shattered early on too as all the older women on the circuit seemed to despise me on sight.

The following week another woman comic turned up. 'If I was to give you any advice at all it's this: don't shag male comedians.'

Later that night Pete said of her, 'I like Nikki but she needs to stop shagging other comedians.'

Nothing about the quality of her jokes or the originality of her material. I wondered if I'd ever find somewhere where women weren't policed or self-policing about who they were riding.

All around me, men were entered into new-act competitions by their wives while silent girlfriends turned up to every gig and watched lovingly from the side of the stage. Boring men with their boring pedestrian material were slapped on the back and nurtured and encouraged all the way into comedy careers. I saw no such thing with women.

In fact, my love of pattern-spotting meant I noticed that the majority of the women who did get the confidence to do a gig tended to hide behind either a musical instrument or a character act.

Still, the comedy circuit was somewhere I immediately felt at ease. The sense of being around people who were more mentally ill than not was immensely comforting. Everything about my personality that made me a problem at university or in most jobs seemed to be treated as some sort of magical power in stand-up.

'You're just *you*!'

A man was grasping me by the arms and beaming into my face backstage. He seemed overjoyed. I'd just come offstage after doing ten minutes at an arts centre in Leeds. The man was Phil Kay, someone who was pretty well known when I was a kid and who was notorious for his chaotic could-be-amazing-could-be-disastrous shows. He looked so excited looking at me as I looked back at him nervously and he said it again: 'You're wonderful because you're just *you*.'

I looked at his feet. He wasn't wearing any shoes.

Chapter Twelve

'Whenever a person shows they're valuable to their game, by being conspicuously virtuous or successful, it's registered by their co-players. Subconsciously, they'll see this person's winning behaviour as a chance to win themselves. They'll desire to learn from them, so they too can rise up in the rankings. This means being near to them as much as possible. As a reward for all their valuable time and knowledge, they'll offer them symbolic status, they lavish them with eye contact and defer to them in conversations; they might maintain a hunched, subservient posture; bare their teeth in submissive displays known as "fear grimaces" in apes and "smiles" in humans.'

—Will Storr, *The Status Game*

By the time I was 25 I'd had somewhere in the region of 50 jobs. I'd been sacked over and over again. Unable to find a template that quite fit me or explained my failures, I applied the 'cool slacker' narrative to myself even though there were just as many positions where I worked hard and tried my best and still got sacked from those as well. I couldn't seem to grasp that office culture is more about *looking* like you're working than actually doing your job well. In one workplace, the boss walked around at 5pm every day smiling and telling everyone, 'Please, go home! Get your dinner! Relax!' Obediently, I'd get up and leave, wondering why no one was listening to him and had their heads in their hands as they continued to look at emails.

'You're not supposed to actually get up and go home,' my colleague whispered to me one evening after he'd left. 'He just likes saying that 'cause it makes *him* look good.'

The autistic comedian Hannah Gadsby pointed out that there aren't many autism-friendly openings for women, claiming that 'the workplace is not suited to us because a lot of the jobs that appeal to our way of thinking are closed off to women or really hostile to them.'[*]

Lots of the jobs that were predominantly held by men didn't require anything like the same number of social calculations as the jobs held by women. All of the jobs that seemed open to me were reliant on my performing femininity correctly – admin roles that involved smiling, showing appropriate deference to male bosses, rubbing along with everyone and wearing uncomfortable clothes. Job interviews were easy. You just did

---

[*]   Christie, J (2019) 'Comedian Hannah Gadsby – how an autism diagnosis changed her life'. *The Scotsman*. www.scotsman.com/whats-on/arts-and-entertainment/comedian-hannah-gadsby-how-autism-diagnosis-changed-her-life-1404790

your hair and makeup nicely and scripted the correct answers to the same questions. A job interview was simply a short bout of intense masking. The moment I had to show up there every day and keep the masking going was always when things fell to bits.

I'd abruptly quit my journalism postgrad in the spring of 2010 to move to Manchester and single-mindedly pursue stand-up. Since being a new comedian paid more in crisps and pints than in money, I'd got an admin job. The office was all women and everyone spoke softly and about an octave higher than me. I was working alongside two specky virgins, Becky and Leanne. I was taking over from a beautiful head-girl type, Lottie, who the two female bosses doted on. She seemed nice until I mentioned in passing that I didn't really have any student debt and she said sweetly, 'Well, yes, because you leach off our taxes, don't you?'* I looked at her, uncertain. Her facial expression didn't match up with the fighting talk that had just come out of her mouth. Long lashes blinked back prettily at me and the corners of her mouth twitched up into a cold smile. I was so slow at processing this sort of thing – the mismatch of facial expression and the intended meaning threw me every time – I'd look dopily at people and say nothing. I marvelled that women could get away with saying the most insulting things as long as they maintained a soft tone of voice. *Just you wait,* I thought. *I'll think of something*

---

* Scottish people don't pay university fees, a policy decision I had no involvement in. I hope Chapters 8 and 9 sufficiently demonstrate that I had a miserable time at university.

really clever to reply to you in about a decade, just as soon as I replay this scenario in my head dozens of times.

It was soon after this interaction that I began to notice the habits of the other two women I worked with. *Pick, slurp, pick, slurp.* Becky was dislodging wet crisps from her back molars before sucking them off her finger then moving on to the next tooth.

Every day without fail at midday, the chorus of *pick, slurp, pick, slurp* began. I knew it was 2pm because Leanne would routinely start weeping quietly in the corner over her workload and everyone else in the office would get up to go pat her back and simper over her. As I looked on, still glued to my chair, I wished more than anything I was capable of communicating my distress in this gentle, palatable way. Instead, I put my headphones back on and blasted industrial metal in my ears to block it all out. I must have been showing some non-verbal signs of misery, though, as my boss came over to my desk and placed a hand on my back. I liked her but she seemed to be doing this with increasing frequency.

'We're like swans,' she smiled. 'We're paddling away frantically under the water but on the surface we're serene.' She said this to me regularly and at no point did I realize she was actually telling me I was useless at my job. A simple, 'You seem stressed; is there anything we can do to help?' would have been more effective.

I began to suspect that I was finding the job stressful because on Saturday mornings I'd wake up to find myself face down on the carpet of my bedroom in my own sick. There was generally an empty bottle of Jack Daniel's next to me. I didn't yet know that I had alexithymia and therefore had little to no insight into my emotional state so tended to have to work backwards. I didn't normally drink to the point of blackout and the only thing that had changed in my life was work. I couldn't understand why it would be distressing me – it was an admin job, I was overqualified for it, it involved little brainpower – so I ignored it and kept gigging every night, drinking more coffee in the day, wringing my hands under my desk at the noise in the office and waking up in my own puke on Saturdays.

'This comedy competition you're in, what's it called – So You Think You're Funny?' Lottie said this to me one day during her work handover to me before she left. 'I looked it up and it's pretty big.'

I nodded. Almost everyone who'd been in the final had gone on to be big pro comedians and on telly.

'Impressive,' she said, sounding faintly annoyed – probably trying to work out how Scottish people were stealing something from her again.

I put my headphones back on. By wearing them, I was unwittingly making reasonable adaptations to my working environment as an autistic person. It didn't interfere with my work as it was a job that simply involved filling out forms and replying to emails. But it didn't *look* good. It *looked* antisocial. They stopped letting me wear the headphones. Swans didn't wear headphones.

For the first time, I spent an afternoon soaking up the sounds of the office, my nerves raw by 4pm. It was especially busy that day and I was tired from gigging four or five nights a week.

Crunch.
Pick.
Slurp.
Crunch.
Pick.
Slurp.

I looked at Becky, willing her to understand how repulsive she was as she sucked another bolus of food from her fingers. Using the last of my reserves to cling, white-knuckled, on to my composure, I stood up, smoothed down the creases in my skirt and walked into the toilets across the hall. They were empty. I kicked a cubicle door and watched it bounce on its hinges. I kicked it again. And again. I rained a load of punches on the door. I just needed to do this for a bit then I could return to the rainforest of disgusting sounds and try and finish my work for the day. As I kicked and kicked like a little carthorse, I felt the stress ease. I could do this.

That was when Jane walked in.

Not long after that I was very gently fired. In a very nice way where the very nice soft-spoken ladies seemed frightened of me.

My mum came to the final of So You Think You're Funny? up in Edinburgh even though I had previously banned her from coming to any gigs. The first one she came to, I'd come off the stage and she'd said faintly, 'You're my daughter . . .' Not a proud, excited, 'You're my daughter!' but a sort of horrified, baffled, 'You're my daughter.' Like she was trying to work out who I was in connection to her.

So when she showed up in Edinburgh I made sure she sat with Lauren and a couple of my other friends, who later reported that she'd cried all the way through and asked repeatedly during the set, 'Am I supposed to find this funny?'

As much as I enjoy repetition you might not so I'll condense the next three years down to this: after about a thousand gigs in grim little pubs across England I got an agent and started getting auditions for TV.

I first got on a panel show by fluke rather than by being intentionally funny. In response to a question I don't remember now, I mentioned that one time in the strip club, Colonel Gaddafi's nephews wanted a lap dance off me. The assembled production staff in their brand-new trainers and nice haircuts in their fancy offices in West London howled laughing as if it was some off-the-wall joke. I smiled and nodded as if I knew what was going on but I thought, *I dunno why everyone's laughing – the Gaddafi lads* did *come in that time.* They'd actually offered me lots of money to have sex with them ('We are the Gaddafi family!' being the main sell) but I thought I better not mention that part.

For you to be bookable on panel shows it should be that if you're dropped in, viewers casually flicking through the channels can look at you and quickly be able to think, *Ah, I know what type of person they are.* So bookers like their gay men to be camp and unthreatening; their working-class people to be coarse and wilfully stupid; if you're brown you need to reaffirm the white viewers' narrow stereotypes about you. Usually, there'll be a resident weirdo – which I naively assumed would be me but because I'm Scottish that had to take precedence over everything and become my main personality trait. Since reading between the lines does not come naturally to me, I didn't understand that when I went on panel shows I was supposed to fall into a very two-dimensional recognizable caricature – mine being 'thick Scotswoman'. But when the host or other panellists jokingly brought up untrue media stereotypes about Scotland and Scottish people I'd reply earnestly, 'That's not true, though,' and it'd have to be edited out. I didn't understand the game.

'I went to Edinburgh uni and I had piano lessons from the age of five,' I protested one time in response to a joke about me being dragged up. Everyone acted like I hadn't said anything and the host swiftly moved on. You're supposed to play along with this both limited and limiting idea of what being working class is but for me the dishonesty of it – the sensation that I was playing into a stereotype to reassure those watching at home that the established power dynamic remained unchanged – was too jarring. My grandfather was a miner who ended up becoming a music teacher with no formal qualifications and used to show me books on the Suzuki method in the hope of turning me into a piano maestro. My mum, a Tesco checkout lady, baked us focaccia, taught herself Spanish in night classes and bought us French-language kids' books from when we were little. My dad obsessed over history and taught me how to draw lifelike portraits. Every time I tried to say a joke about us being deep-fried-Mars-bar-eating troglodytes, I'd picture my relatives and the lie of it stuck in my mouth.

I decided I'd watch everyone and copy them as best I could until the autism had been rubbed off me and I was cured. I started to feel excited about the day when I wouldn't have any autism because I'd have learned every rule, hacked every social scenario.

I started to feel tired a lot. I made sure I wrote some jokes into my set that referenced my tiredness as I was finding it increasingly difficult to hide onstage. I'd achieved the dream and escaped the traditional world of work for the arts but still had little clue what was going on in 90 per cent of work meetings.

'So, what's this meeting about?' I said to a comedy producer as we sat in a booth of the theatre I'd just performed in. I eyed the other two producers warily as they queued at the bar. I'd just done an hour's show and I didn't really want to be there as I preferred to go home straight after.

'Oh, this isn't a meeting; this is just us having a friendly drink.' He sounded hurt.

I tried my best to make my face into a smile but it felt too tight. None of us were friends and we all only knew each other because in different ways we were all involved with each other in a work capacity. Our backgrounds and ages were all wildly different and none of us would ever socialize in the normal world but for some reason we had to pretend we were great pals.

'So we're not having a meeting about the script?' I asked.

'Oh well, yeah we can chat about the script, of course.'

He said this like it had just occurred to him. In TV, people

247

wore casual clothes and went for drinks and swore and gossiped but it was all a trick mirror. I learned that when everyone was acting casual you were still basically being interviewed for a job.* I learned that it was important to start pretending to love everyone.

'Oh, I *love* so and so!' I'd say about people I despised. It made me feel unwell.

'Give me the Xanax,' I said, holding my hand outstretched.

My boyfriend, Conor, shook his head stubbornly. Our bedroom was trashed, drawers upended, suitcases raided as I'd tried to find my secret stash.

'They're not in the house anymore,' he said quietly.

'Give me my *Xanax*!'

'You're really frightening me.'

'FUCKING GIVE ME THEM THEN.'

I'd started to notice recently that the urge to say, 'Give me the Xanax!' really overrode the embarrassment of saying the sentence upwards of 50 times. It felt easily solved. If he'd just

---

* In *The Class Ceiling* (2019; Policy Press), sociologist Sam Friedman coined the term 'studied informality' to describe how the TV industry obscures hierarchies through bosses dressing informally and work meetings taking place in pubs under the guise of 'casual chats'. I think this blurring of the power dynamics impacts autistic people just as much as those from working-class backgrounds. Powerful people in TV tend to actively play down their high status, which creates a mess of confusion for people whose neurotype struggles to accept social hierarchies.

give me the Xanax, which was all I wanted in this life, I'd feel better and we could all relax and stop trashing the house.

'Fern, I think you have a problem with this.'

I didn't have a problem with it. In fact, I thought Xanax was the thing I'd been missing my whole life. I'd been filming a series that involved travelling around Europe and one of the crew gave me a couple for the flight. I remember how quickly it kicked in and knocked me off my feet. The constant worry and fear and pain from noise and light and other people disappeared completely. The drug also stripped away any ability or desire to mask and I remember the horror on my friend's face as he saw me shout at an old German man who stood too close to me in the airport queue. Then the pill went *flump* on my brain like a big marshmallow duvet and I slept peacefully all the way home.

When I got home the crew member who'd given me the pill gave me a weird email address and I ordered an enormous amount of the anti-anxiety drug from some faceless dealer in Spain. With Xanax, I didn't do the furniture-smashing thing when I got home from work. As soon as I felt the urge kick in, I could take a little blue pill and be unconscious within half an hour. I felt really proud that I'd found a solution to my bouts of blind rage.

'Please,' I begged Conor, my voice breaking. 'Can I just have it? This is the only thing that makes me happy so please just give me it.' Conor shook his head.

Then, getting angry, I replied: 'It's mine, you cunt! You don't own it!'

This was all still pre-diagnosis. No one knew why I smashed

furniture. The friends I'd confided in looked uncomfortable. The useless therapist didn't have an answer. Even NHS psychiatrists couldn't tell me anything. So why not just live under a big chemical blanket between now and death? I couldn't seem to change my weird unnamed behaviours and no one else was coming to save me. Sometimes the old useless instinct that my parents would help would kick in and I'd mention it to Dad when he visited by showing him where I'd punched the cupboards or torn a door off its hinges and he'd look past me to a corner of the room and whistle or say, 'Oh.'

Self-medicating with whatever was available, I started taking Ritalin (bought from the same dealer) in the day to balance out the Xanax. It reminded me of Provigil, an anti-narcolepsy drug I'd taken (again, unprescribed) at university to concentrate on my dissertation but now took just because.

I had just been knocked back from another panel show and the commissioner wanted a chat with me over the phone.

'We *love* you but we thought you didn't have enough screen time under your belt.'

This was confusing as the only way of getting more screen time was for them to put me on screen more. I thought of the person they'd picked over me. She was rail-thin and effortlessly beautiful. I slapped a hand to my forehead, suddenly understanding the assignment.

'Do you want me to lose weight and get a nose job?' I offered. I'd broken my nose years ago after enthusiastically opening a door into my own face, an injury no one who hadn't witnessed it believed as most people take stuff like spatial awareness and hand-eye coordination for granted.

There was a pause as she decided how to take this. She laughed, uncertainly. 'Hahaha! See, this is what we *love* about you, Fern!'

I remained deadly serious. 'But I will if you want me to.'

She laughed again, more uncomfortable this time.

I thought for a moment about how much they loved me – enough to not put me on television. I wondered why she was laughing when I'd just offered to make myself more telegenic. I understood now that it was important for me to be thin and pretty for them. I was offering to be the best for the job.

Over and over again, the same confusing answer came up when I auditioned for shows.

'We like Fern, just not for this series. It's important to get the mix right.'

A mysterious thing called 'the mix' came up a lot in casting panel shows. It was tricky getting the right mix for utterly meaningless shit that was of no consequence to anyone.

'We feel Fern would be better for the second series.'

I checked my calendar. The second series was coming up in October so I'd be sure to keep my diary free and clear. Conor asked if I'd like to go on holiday in autumn. I shook my head immediately, rubbing my hands together anxiously and staring at my laptop screen.

'As long as it's not October because that's when the second series is recording and all these producers said I'd be a good fit for the second series.'

He paused, as if he were unsure of whether to say something.

'Fern. I don't work in TV so I'm not an expert by any means but . . . You know how people say this to you a lot, well – they don't *literally* mean they want you on the second series.'

I froze. '. . . What?'

'It's a kind way of letting you down gently.'

'Are you fucking joking?'

I tried to work out how lying to someone's face was a kindness.

It was around this point that I began to come to terms with the fact that we were all playing a game where everyone was supposed to be thin and pretty but we were meant to lie about it. I stressed about what I was ordering on a job as nothing was safe to eat. An actress on set noticed me shaking my head over the menu, as I got more and more flustered.

'Oh, do you watch what you eat?' She was thin and exercised a lot. I was confused. Were we supposed to pretend we didn't care? TV sets were filled with boxes and boxes of uneaten doughnuts and sandwiches. Everyone successful was always on a mad diet that involved not eating after 6pm or only eating until 3pm but if you copied them and mentioned that you were on a diet too everyone got inexplicably weird.

I went home to Conor and told him. I was now heavily reliant on Conor to translate any social situation I didn't understand.

'They *are* dieting but they don't want you to mention it as it makes people sad. The TV industry doesn't want to feel responsible for making you worried about your weight.'

'But they are the reason? And they give all the jobs to beautiful thin people?'

'Yes, but you're not supposed to say that out loud.' He thought for a moment before adding: 'No one wants to feel a throwaway comment is responsible for someone else feeling terrible.'

I shook my head. This was a new level of bullshit. I started going to the gym four times a week and when people asked what I was doing I shrugged and did the neurotypical thing of pretending it was effortless. 'I just avoid alcohol,' I said, omitting that I counted every calorie and exercised to the point that it was sometimes hard to do my job as I was so exhausted.

I wished I could go back to being fat and happy but it was simple social economics – I didn't have the social currency to be fat. I wasn't likeable. I couldn't charm people. I'd no social intuition. Nothing about me put people at ease. The least I could do was be thin; anything else was putting myself at an unnecessary disadvantage. If you're prepared to be thin you will be rewarded with money and status – and from what I could see, both were in short supply for most autistic women.

Chapter Thirteen

'Though masking is incredibly taxing and causes us
a lot of existential turmoil, it's rewarded and facilitated
by neurotypical people. Masking makes autistic people
easier to "deal" with.'

—Devon Price, *Unmasking Autism*

'Can I have less hairspray? It's just my thing,' I muttered to
myself, practising making it sound convincing as I brushed my
teeth readying myself for another day's filming.

'Instead of saying fluorescent lights give you meltdowns, say
instead that you have a migraine. You can't come out as autistic
to everyone – that in itself can be exhausting.' This is how Sue
explained it to me when she gave me a new kind of therapy
that involved teaching me how to relearn my way of being
autistic, which had for too long involved me hiding my stress
for everyone else's benefit at the cost of my own health.

It's 2022 as I write this and I'm still waiting to find someone I respect to speak openly and in detail about meltdowns. I'm really annoyed that I have to be the one to do this. I want to keep getting work and I want people to continue to fancy me and by talking about this I'm likely torpedoing my career as well as any future shagging prospects. If there was a magic pill I could take to stop them I would sell my house to pay for it.

'I had a meltdown' means something completely different for neurotypical people. For your average person it conjures up an image of a woman getting panicked at work over a deadline and having an outburst in the office. Maybe she has a little cry in the toilets after. It's tricky to use exactly the same word to communicate the electrical shitstorm that seizes my brain and musculoskeletal system when I have a meltdown.

Before my diagnosis only a handful of people were aware that I had meltdowns and no one other than my partner and our deeply traumatized cat knew the extent to which they had an impact on my everyday life. I rarely try and explain them because they are so baffling to neurotypicals that the moment you say 'smashing up furniture' you can see the horror in their eyes as they decide which anger-management problem you have. If anyone saw me having one my career would be over in a flash but there's no point in me writing a book about autism then skipping over the least-discussed part of being autistic. Prior to diagnosis I didn't even have a word for what was happening to me. My browser history was filled with endless searches for 'Why do I smash up my house?', 'Why do I punch things when I'm not angry?' and 'Punching things for no reason!'

An autistic meltdown is when you ignore your sensory overstimulation – whether that's a build-up of noise, lights, socializing or uncertainty – become dysregulated and lose control of your brain, speech, body and movements.

When they happen to me, I generally shout and break stuff, repeating the same words or the same question over and over again. I cannot stress this enough: it looks fucking mental. I'm very aware – painfully aware – of how insane it looks when I get locked inside my body. But I have to step back and wait for it to play out. Resisting them tends to prolong them. Really, I have very little to do with it. I'm a tiny machine operator perched in the top of my head and I have to surrender control, raising my hands in despair and watching helplessly while the machine rampages all around me. Tutting at the destruction, I peer out and can see through the windows of my eyes that I'm punching a plug socket over and over while my boyfriend says gently, 'Yes, yes, ask the same question over and over,' but it sounds pretty distant as if everything's very far away.

Afterwards, I'll take to my bed feeling totally wiped out. The rest of the day is a write-off and any dinner plans will have to be scrapped as I return to eating bland samefoods.*

---

* 'Samefoods' is a term used by the autistic community to describe the often bland, safe foods we eat to regulate ourselves. If your sensory system is overstimulated then it makes sense to down-regulate your system by eating plain beige foods. Some autistics exist solely on their samefoods, which can make aspects of everyday life – socializing or eating out at restaurants, for example – tricky. Personally I only revert to eating this way during periods of uncertainty or disruptions to my routine.

There seems to be a decent number of autistic women speaking about shutdowns, the less offensive sister of meltdowns. In the documentary *I Am Greta*, Greta Thunberg goes mute, overwhelmed by the climate crisis, and sits on the ground hunched over while her dad tries to comfort her. Even though I occasionally have shutdowns, which have often been misinterpreted by those around me as a ploy or a sulk, I do wonder: as a woman, if I'd been the shutdown-type of autistic, how much longer would it have taken for me to get diagnosed? Shutdowns aren't disruptive; oftentimes those around you may not even be aware anything's up. When a meltdown happens you *know* something's seriously wrong. People around me have been so deeply disturbed by my meltdowns and anything that looked like explosive female anger[*] that I've been compelled to keep seeking answers.

People will overlook or ignore our perceived deficits for as long as they can make money out of us but when we meltdown, when we stop fulfilling the misleading label of 'high functioning' through failing to perform 'normal' for them (often due to a lack of reasonable accommodations for a disability society barely acknowledges is real), there is very little compassion.[†]

*

---

[*] Though it's important to point out here that a meltdown is not an expression of anger but of extreme anxiety, like a huge fight-or-flight response.

[†] A good example of this is James Damore's sacking from Google: www.theguardian.com/technology/2017/nov/16/james-damore-google-memo-interview-autism-regrets

Whenever I meet autistics who were diagnosed at much younger ages and received the correct support, I can't stop thinking bitterly about whether things could have been different for me if I'd been diagnosed at a younger age instead of artificially socialized as allistic. Maybe by now, in my thirties, I'd know how to live in a way that avoided meltdowns instead of having the maladaptive coping mechanisms of a non-verbal two-year-old. But hey, the important thing is that I can do a reasonably convincing impression of a normal woman so as not to make anyone around me uncomfortable. Increasingly, though, the trade-off has stopped seeming like a good deal.

Ideally, we learn how to identify our pre-meltdown stage – known as the 'rumble' stage – and try to take steps to prevent it from happening. For me, 35 years of having meltdowns in secret and discussing them with no one means they are as much a reflex to me as breathing.

They creep up on me without warning. Say I'm busy and have been working six or seven days a week for several months with no end in sight. Between a meeting and an evening's gig I will get my nails done for a TV taping, something I don't care about but have come to understand I'm meant to do. It's dark outside the salon and looking at my reflection in the window, I make sure to adjust my hunched posture (I don't want to look autistic, which involves constantly monitoring how autistic I look on a scale of 1 to 10). I admire how, even though I feel like an alien in a meat suit, from the outside all anyone walking past the salon will see is a normal professional lady. I have even bought a Completely Normal Woman™ handbag despite the fact I hate handbags and it's too small to put anything useful in. I zone out while the manicurist gets to work removing and reapplying polish but I quickly come to with a jolt as I realize she's inexplicably cut my nails down to the quick before polishing them. I feel some dismay and confusion but pay her and rush to my gig. About an hour later I'm trying to enjoy a friend's set but the sensation that my fingertips are raw triggers the grotesque feeling that the inside of my body is being exposed to the outside. It's then that a terrible gloomy foreboding sweeps over me. I attempt to ignore it and try to concentrate on the performance but my chest continues to tighten and in the privacy of darkness I start to clench and unclench my fists rapidly. I look down at my nails and realize again she's cut them completely off, right down to the nailbeds. I feel the same helpless fury you feel when you get a micro fringe and know no amount of rage will make the hair grow back immediately.

By the time I'm on the train home, and with nothing to distract me from the sensation of my raw fingers, I'm crawling out my skin. Feeling a prickle start up all over my body, I try to scratch my face; but with no nails, the fingertips and their pillowy nailbeds just rub disgustingly against my face, now impotent against the itch. I reach my house 30 minutes later and the sensation of raw pink flesh has become unbearable and my breathing more and more shallow. Anticipating a meltdown, I smoke weed to try and halt it while still in the rumble stage. Conor comes through to the bedroom and lies on top of me hugging me, a human weighted blanket. That seems to help a bit. I smoke more weed and go to the spare room to try and sleep, thinking, *Distractions, distractions* . . . I'm certain I've read somewhere that I should distract myself with other sensations like rubbing hand lotion into my hands but the thought of piling more sensation onto my hands right now makes me want to puke.

I can't help but furiously think back to that bitch of a manicurist, imagining the negative Tripadvisor review I'll leave for them before realizing that no one else going to the nail salon is a lunatic and underpaid Vietnamese manicurists can't very well be expected to cater to the sensory needs of an undercover autistic. Instead, I rack my brain for what helps in these scenarios and what I've learned in therapy about stopping a meltdown in the rumble stage. In need of a distracting sensation, I grab makeup wipes and start to furiously scrub my face clean. I start to scream quietly so as not to wake Conor up. I scrub in rhythmic circles, the sensation of raw pink nailbeds refusing to go away. If anything, the weed is making the mental image of my exposed hands loom large in the dark. I scrub my forehead before remembering I just had Botox last week and I'm now moving the Botox around and I will end up with one eyebrow higher than the other, and then everyone will see that I've failed in my efforts to be a proper woman once again. I cry-scream. I scratch my legs with my nubs of nails. I scratch so hard I leave long stripy bruises. Defeated, I give up fighting the meltdown, walk into the bathroom and swoop everything off the glass shelf before promptly falling asleep.

The following morning, I have another meltdown within 15 minutes of waking up. Conor puts in the reasonable request that I clean up the exploded handwash on the bathroom floor. I do so and the sensation and smell of the viscous goop touching my raw fingers leads me to walk off to another room to do some screaming. As I scream, I accept I will likely never make friends with the people renting next door. I pack my gym stuff (the gym being a thing I do to try and prevent meltdowns) and dress for work, screaming and swearing to myself intermittently. It's 8am and already I feel totally depleted. The doorbell goes and I remember the builder is here to do our ensuite. Panting and trying to shake the nervous energy out of my arms by waving them about, I practise a rigid 1950s-housewife grin before taking a deep breath and flinging the front door open.

'Hiyaaaa! Do you want a tea?'

On the platform at the train station, I calmly consider flinging myself under the next train. Not in a 'woe is me' way – the thought presents itself very coolly, offering itself up as a logical solution. I'm just so *over* these and when I think of living the rest of my life with meltdowns the very thought is too tiring, too sad, too much. I look at my phone and run through the last ten people I texted. There is literally no one in my life I can talk to about this. I stare at the train tracks again and idly speculate about how many women have killed themselves over meltdowns, having no words to identify what was happening to them.

I look for help online and as usual am forced to read guides for parents of autistic children. An article I find explains that they (we) feel our fingernails to be an extension of ourselves, therefore the cutting of them causes acute sensory distress. These pamphlets offer little in the way of help to me, the adult autistic, and are more about how parents should manage their unruly autistic child. There is nothing online for adults with sensory problems even though all those kids they write the advice for have to grow up at some point.

I go to the gym, lifting my bodyweight in iron over and over again. I think back to something I've read about needing more proprioceptive stimulation* and how weightlifting is one of the things I'm supposed to do (unsurprisingly, I was drawn to it long before diagnosis). Autistics generally require more proprioceptive input. The difference in our brains means our vestibular system is skewed and off-kilter and so we often don't have a good sense of where our body ends and the world begins. I fell over a lot (I had to quit running after repeatedly falling out of nowhere and snapping my ankle twice), had poor fine motor skills and constantly felt like I was made of jelly. A way to redress this imbalance is by increasing your sensory input by doing stuff like push-ups, using weighted blankets, chewing gum and pushing and pulling heavy stuff around. Had I been diagnosed at school I would've been taught all of this by an occupational therapist but instead I've had to learn on my own through trial and error that for me: light touch is bad, heavy touch is good.

I realize I'm unable to make eye contact or small talk with my trainer as I normally do and I feel I'm about to cry at any moment. My masking ability has been drained from back-to-back meltdowns. I follow my doctor's advice and lie to my trainer and say I didn't sleep well last night as this is something allistics understand and won't make them feel uncomfortable. I ignore

---

* Proprioception is a person's sense of their body's movement and position and is sometimes known as the 'sixth sense'. Many people with autism seek proprioceptive input to help regulate their responses to sensory stimuli.

the instinct to cry and instead concentrate on making my whole body rigid, pulling my rounded shoulders back and deadlifting 100kg. The lift requires all my concentration. Afterwards, I walk along the Thames enjoying the cold sun bouncing off the river and realize with cautious glee the weightlifting has made the horrible sensation in my hands go away.

By that evening, the positive effect wears off and, because my nails can't grow back in a day and I can't handle the sensation, I have a further three meltdowns, breaking a personal record and Conor's remaining goodwill. That night, I lie in bed biting my hand as hard as I can to stop myself from going downstairs, grabbing the pliers from the toolbox and tearing my nails off completely. I check Instagram. I have appeared on a teatime quiz show and men are talking about my lovely long legs and how sexy I am. I wonder how sexy they'd think I was if they saw me here biting the back of my hand like a maniac, screaming and clenching my fists in despair as I google how many millimetres nails grow back in a week. The following day, unable to lose one more day of work to the sensation of the glossy shellac on my stubby boy-nails and desperate to regain some sense of control, I go to another salon and have the polish removed.

Imagine going through this in secret. For years. Imagine no one in psychiatry telling you what is happening to you. No one in your family. You can't even begin to tell your friends. Worse, imagine *telling* people. Telling people that something as basic as a manicure ends up writing off a week of your life.

*

The idea that meltdowns are manipulative is absurd and a cause of gross misunderstanding between autistics and the rest of the world. If my meltdowns were in any way manipulative I'd ensure I had one every time someone in the industry asked to meet me for a general chat. My meltdowns are comparable to explosive diarrhoea – I can just about hold them in until I get home and can do it in private but occasionally I lose control and shit myself in public.

For a public meltdown to be merely embarrassing is currently the best-case scenario. Too often we get attacked or even killed during them by police untrained and unsympathetic to the chaos that's playing out in our nervous system. In 2018, Courtney Topic, a 22-year-old with no prior history of violence and who had previously described being unable to read facial expressions, was shot dead by Sydney police while in a hypervigilant, hyperaroused meltdown state when she waved a knife at onlookers.[*]

And in 2016, trans man Kayden Clarke, who had bravely tried to spread awareness of what meltdowns looked like by sharing a video online of his support dog calming him during one, was shot dead by police in Arizona when they were called out during a suicide attempt.[†]

If you're black and autistic it gets worse. Many people will be

---

[*]   www.theguardian.com/australia-news/2018/jul/30/police-tactics-entirely-inappropriate-in-shooting-death-of-courtney-topic-says-coroner

[†]   www.independent.co.uk/news/world/americas/woman-with-asperger-s-syndrome-who-shared-viral-dog-video-shot-dead-by-police-in-arizona-a6855901.html

familiar with the story of Elijah McClain, who was stopped by police in Colorado for wearing headphones and dancing in the street. Even after clearly advocating for himself by saying, 'I'm an introvert. I'm just different . . .' he was suffocated and over-sedated, causing him to go into cardiac arrest on the pavement; he died six days later. In 2013 in Illinois an eight-year-old black girl was handcuffed and shackled during a meltdown while in 2020 in Sydney, Australia a nine-year-old girl was also handcuffed by police during a meltdown.[*,†]

These incidents are equivalent to punishing and arresting someone having an epileptic seizure. People used to think seizures were demonic possession or that the sufferer was under the influence of black magic. The treatment of autistic adults having meltdowns today is so staggeringly behind every other area of disability rights that it seems we've barely emerged from the dark ages.

The autism influencer Lauren Melissa Elzey, who posts under the username 'autienelle' on Instagram, has pointed out that meltdowns are more likely to be caused by those prone to black-and-white thinking, observing 'black-and-white thinking is often used to describe a common autistic trait. This specific trait revolves around autistics taking a stance and sticking to it.

---

[*] atlantablackstar.com/2013/03/08/eight-year-old-special-needs-student-arrested-in-illinois/

[†] 9news.com.au/national/nine-year-old-girl-with-autism-handcuffed-by-police-in-sydney-after-school-meltdown/7020af65-f087-445e-858a-b0137dbad4d4

While some refer to this as rigidity, autistics may not experience it as such.'*

This made a lot of sense to me as my perfectionism left me in a state of rigidity that meant there was no room to fail, no room for things to be any way other than my way, and consequently my brain was panicking all the time. The harder I worked the more I was priming my mind and body into the perfect state for a meltdown.

Starting in January 2020, I tracked mine meticulously for a year and found they weren't caused by furniture being moved, as I had thought, but commonly by disrupted sleep, build-up of external noise and light, excessive masking, smoking weed, drinking alcohol and hormonal changes in the week before my period.

Reducing meltdowns became a full-time job wherein I was both the scientist and the lab rat. I managed to reduce them to the point that I was having them only in the week leading up to my period, where I'd feel defeated.

Even excessive excitement caused meltdowns. When the rights for this book went into a heated auction I was the most excited I'd been in my life. I had daily meltdowns for a week and consequently booked in for a therapy session.

'You have to understand the body registers excitement the same way it registers anxiety,' Sue explained.

As she said it, I thought back to all the times I'd been so

---

* askaspienelle.wordpress.com/2021/12/28/meltdowns-and-black
  -white-thinking/

excited to see Conor after a stretch away on tour that I'd had a meltdown within minutes of seeing him and ruined everything.

'It's all arousal of the nervous system.'

Sue told me about spoon theory, which started as a way for sufferers of chronic illness to explain their limited energy levels to those around them but has since become popular as a way of explaining autistic energy levels to ourselves and those close to us. Embarrassingly, I took this literally, assuming it to be some sort of fixed currency that had the exact same values for everyone. I had to start realizing that the more I used all my spoons up, the more I was guaranteed to have a meltdown that day.

Things that drain my spoons are: noisy bars, fluorescent lighting, most conversations with fake people, work meetings. Things that increase them are: being alone, listening to music on my headphones, watching the same TV show for the millionth time, playing with my cats, smoking weed.*

'What about walking?' Sue said one day.

'Um. I like walking, yeah.'

I wasn't sure where she was going with this. I was pretty sure I mainly walked to lose weight.

'It's just that some people find the repetition of it can be helpful.' I thought about this for a moment. I considered how much happier I was when I was working in Scotland because

---

* You may have noticed I mentioned earlier that weed is one of the causes of my meltdowns; but cannabis seems to act as both a help and a hindrance for different aspects of autism. See for example: www.ncbi.nlm.nih.gov/pmc/articles/PMC6336869/

I walked everywhere at night and realized that the walking in itself was the thing. I thought of happy memories of times I'd left gigs at Battersea Arts Centre in south-west London on foot and walked all across south London to get home. I'd walked and walked and felt peace. The gigs themselves had been terrible but if I walked long enough it was like balm for my brain.

I took Sue's advice and walked and walked, rubbing my fingers and thumbs together as I did so, flapping my hands, no longer caring if anyone thought it looked weird. Stimming wasn't the gross thing I'd thought it was and anyway, no one in London cares or looks at what anyone does. Sure enough, the meltdowns subsided. I barely noticed until Conor texted me one day: 'You've been really good lately. I'm proud of you.'

I also exercised regularly to prevent meltdowns but found that even too much of that actually caused them. Lifting very heavy weights, for example, can cause overload in the central nervous system. *Of course*, I thought to myself. I made the connection there and then that *everything* in my thinking towards meltdowns had to be related to the nervous system and sensory system. Excited by my experiment now, I started mixing up my exercise routine. I'd always despised yoga classes, with their competitive women and espousal of pseudo-spiritual woo and Eastern spirituality while the clientele wore £90 yoga pants. I scrapped the cynicism and started thinking of yoga as moving meditation and preventative treatment for meltdowns. This shift in perspective helped and the frequency and severity of the meltdowns reduced yet again.

I joined CrossFit, reasoning I'd love it as it involved intensive sessions of weightlifting every day and I liked weightlifting. I hated it more than any exercise since school. My coordination was worse than normal and for the first time in years I fell over when I was doing lifts. I started to dread attending, to dread scripting my hello to the chirpy woman on the desk as I entered, to dread talking to the manic type-A people who loved box jumps and high-fiving after endless burpees. Then I realized: most people loved the community aspect of CrossFit. They *loved* the group element. If I'd learned anything about myself in the year since being diagnosed it was that I don't do well in communities. Socializing while at a gym was pointlessly draining energy that could be better used elsewhere. I went to the gym primarily to build up my energy, so it was counter-intuitive to go to a gym environment with excessive noise or social demands when I could spend that energy on the workout itself.

When you have a nervous system that's in a state of hyperarousal, muscles that stiffen into knots every week and lungs that breathe shallowly every day, you start viewing exercise as a necessity. I stopped viewing yoga as crap pretend exercise and started seeing it as something I needed to regulate my breathing, to force a mind–body connection where alexithymia had left me numb. I viewed intense exercise as a way of putting fake stress on my body so it could better cope with the very real anxiety it felt every day. Weightlifting stopped me falling and tripping as regularly and gave me a more solid sense of myself (I mean this very literally – non-autistics speak about exercise very differently). Putting on muscle has helped my body feel more concrete, less likely to fall over.

A few months after diagnosis I went for a drink with my agents. One of them went to the bar and the other one looked around cautiously before asking: 'Are you still – and this may be embarrassing to ask – are you still smashing up the furniture and stuff?'

'I got really great therapy and it fixed everything,' I lied. I knew it was the more comforting thing to say, for both of us perhaps. It was unlikely he wanted to hear about my careful tracking of meltdown data and how certain months saw a spike and other months saw a fall and that I had to work through every single influencing factor until I could find a cure, since the NHS didn't seem to know or care. I couldn't be bothered to explain to him that all I wanted was for my meltdowns to be less expensive and involve fewer trips to B&Q after I'd kicked holes in the walls and that just reducing them to once a month would be a dream come true.

Six months in and the year of tracking meltdowns seemed to be paying off. I used my autism to spot patterns in what caused them and was certain I'd find the solution.

By August I was down to a miraculous zero, which I suspected was because I was living alone in a friend's empty flat in Glasgow while I put a new tour show together. I knew now for a fact, no matter how much Conor insisted otherwise, that living alone was better for me. I had always believed without question what parents and boyfriends had told me was best for me. But now I had the data that proved otherwise. I told Sue about it and she agreed it was true that many autistics found it easier to live alone. The downside to living alone would be that I would stop normal eating and sleeping patterns. When I was around Conor I copied what he ate and slept when he slept. If I wasn't tired at night, I'd still lie next to him and pretend to be asleep and after the first year of dating the sleep problems I'd had my whole life significantly decreased. It was absurd that you could just copy what the other person in your house was doing and it would make life more normal, more stable.

By October they shot up dramatically and I charted seven in a month, a record high since diagnosis. I was back to working flat out with no end in sight. I asked to cut back on some jobs but this didn't happen so I was forced to cut out most socializing instead. I thought of the time Stephen Fry had a manic episode and abruptly left the West End play he was starring in to board a ferry to France. This seemed like an appealing option.

I observed myself like this was a scientific experiment. All the conditions were as they should be. I was following all the advice. I had cut out alcohol and weed, was taking Vitamins D and B, magnesium, ashwagandha and 5-HTP. I was walking 10,000 steps a day, going to yoga and Pilates, weightlifting, eating at regular times, stimming more openly, masking less. Still the meltdowns came, often relentlessly and one day after another. I looked again at my data. I was forced to conclude it was excessive work. Yet again I promised myself: *Just get through these three months then try and work less* – even though by now I knew it was a lie.

In November I had ten. I was preparing to start filming *Taskmaster* and the stress of prep along with my usual workload was taking its toll. I asked to cut one job from my schedule – a podcast – but had to do more episodes so as not to be in breach of contract. I started to have meltdowns in front of people – including in the studio, where I tried to discreetly hit myself in the head over and over during a recording while my co-host tried to politely look away. The problem is that neurotypicals interpret this as rage when actually it's more akin to someone slapping an analogue telly that's on the blink. When I hit myself in the head, I'm trying to knock my nervous system back into function.

December. Month 12. I *should* have been cured by now. I went to Tesco with Conor to buy a Christmas tree. While we looked for tinsel and mulled wine, a woman started singing 'Last Christmas' and the high-pitched whine tuned everything out like a fly buzzing overhead. The syrupy *X Factor* crooning synced up with the flickering fluorescent lights in the ceiling. I felt the tiny hairs in my ear stand on end. I thought to myself that people who sang in public should be fined on the spot. People who whistled anywhere outside their private property should have their lips stapled shut. I stood motionless in the aisle, put one hand over my ear and grimaced. Conor pulled me away gently by the elbow. I asked to buy some chocolate. Conor awkwardly reminded me I'd ordered him to stop me from doing this because I was dieting for filming. I had a meltdown and started punching bars of Dairy Milk over and over. I remembered a work colleague who once told me I didn't look autistic and thought, *Look at me now, fucker.*

In therapy later with Sue on Zoom, our respective Christmas trees twinkling in the background, I sat with my head in my hands and told her again I couldn't seem to fix the meltdowns. She told me that in the same way you get As, Bs and Cs at school, I needed to grade my progress on reducing meltdowns that way. Currently I was giving myself either an A or a U grade with nothing in between.

I'd met with *Taskmaster* producers before we started filming in December. Someone asked: 'Are there any phobias you have that might get in the way of filming?' I paused and thought about what Sue said and considered whether I should openly say I'm autistic or do what she advised – half-mask and tell a white lie to explain my sensory problems. I looked at their kind faces. I so wanted to please them and do a good job.

'Honestly, anything that might be an issue for you, it's better you tell us now. We've had a few people on the show frightened of balloons and didn't tell us then they freaked out on the day.'

A balloon phobia was pretty mental. Maybe I could tell them? I thought of the money I was being paid and the inevitable confusion on their faces if I explained that too much light or noise would cause me to go from normal to mute. How stupid and precious that would sound. Trying to encourage myself, I tried to think of what a positive experience I'd had telling the producers on another series I'd filmed.

'Erm, I'm a bit funny with fluorescent lights and some noises . . .' I trailed off, embarrassed. What was I going to say? 'Oh, and if I get overloaded I'll have a meltdown that looks like something a toddler might do. Or I'll stop speaking and making eye contact and I'll lose my ability to make you think I'm a semi-normal person.'

I thought again of the money. It was a lot and I wanted a new kitchen. They could still replace me at this stage. 'But no phobias, no,' I said finally.

We all laughed. Inside my head, I pressed 'play' on the sound of an engine revving up – the sound I always made inside my brain when I was getting ready to do some hardcore masking. I could spend the money I was earning on more fancy therapy.

I figured if I could make enough money before I was 40 and had the career-ending nervous breakdown I seemed to be hurtling towards, I could retire and go live as a hermit back home in Scotland. Masking was surely better than being poor? When I got home, I composed an email to my agent to say I'd tried to explain my autism to them so that it wasn't an issue, hoping for some advice on what to do. I stopped typing, read it back and saved it to my drafts folder. The pool of people I can talk to about this is so small it's barely a puddle. I thought of a couple of high-profile comics I vaguely know who've had breakdowns from overwork and wondered if I should talk to them. It felt too risky so I decided against it.

On the first day of filming, I mentally totted up all the normal things I'd said throughout the day. During the tasks I'd unmasked and was my true autistic self. *Taskmaster* was unintentionally the most autism-friendly job I'd ever had because it's a show that values being yourself. By then I'd learned I was my very worst self when concentrating on hiding my autism – so that meant that the only way forward was to openly stim, rubbing my hands together like a little praying mantis, while I thought of how to solve tasks. I'd opted to say my first instinct rather than focus on the correct thing to say and was encouraged when it was met with laughs instead of derision. I felt a very pure happiness that I didn't feel in the hellish forced group banter of panel shows.

The following day I went in to have my makeup done by a new makeup artist. In a way, I like meeting new people as it means every day is a new opportunity to redeem yourself, to make a fresh start at being seen as a normal woman and practise at it. It's when people get to know you that they realize something's seriously off and that's harder to rectify.

Wanting her to like me, I thought of some safe small talk for women. An article[*] I'd recently read online suddenly popped into my head.

'Have you seen the new *Sex and the City* spin-off?'

'Ooh yes, it's not very good is it. Not the same without Samantha.'

I lit up. 'Right? You know SJP bullied her off the set?'

'Oh?'

'Yeah, and if you look at the Instagram posts around the time of the second film, she made all these weird comments. Also, Cynthia Nixon and SJP were old friends and they ganged up on her when they made the Atlantic City episode in Season 3 by renting a house without her and—'

I couldn't stop now. The persecution of Kim Cattrall and her potential ostracization from a group of mean girls was too appealing to remind myself *not to monologue*. I took the makeup artist through my dossier of evidence that SJP was a cow. I added that SJP didn't see it like that and had issued her own statement on the matter, then realized she'd gone quiet.

'Wow. You really do like the series, don't you?'

Ah no. I'd failed. I can get interested in the same things as regular women but I will inevitably end up showing my enthusiasm autistically and neurotypicals are uncomfortable with this. My research tells me they find it creepy and unnerving.

---

[*]   www.cosmopolitan.com/entertainment/tv/a35246263/kim-cattrall
      -sarah-jessica-parker-drama-timeline/

I clammed up and let her tong my hair in silence. I've a tendency to spend hours, weeks or months agonizing over conversations, wondering how I could've performed 'normal' better, but had decided that this habit also had to go as part of my mission to reduce meltdowns. I've also had to consciously train myself out of feeling bad for not masking and feeling shame for seeming autistic. To do so adds unnecessary stress, which results in – you've guessed it – more meltdowns. So ironically the harder I try to hide my autism, the more I'll end up being visibly autistic.

There's no neat happy ending here. I still have to half-mask at work. Still, the more I 'came out' as autistic or half-masked, the less I felt revolted at my odd posture or voice; and in turn, the more I stood up for myself the calmer I felt. The calmer I felt, the more the meltdowns reduced further. Learning how to cope with them came only in part from my therapist – mostly it came from the radical autism-acceptance movement that is growing online among late-diagnosed women and non-binary folk. It did not come from my GP or a psychiatrist. While it's great I had access to this information, put together by a group of people who are built to learn every possible fact on a topic, it should not be the case that I'm having to learn how to cope as a newly diagnosed person from 19-year-old girls on TikTok. Is it right that when I felt completely isolated in those first few months after diagnosis, my first source of information was podcasts created by other late-diagnosed autistic women who, like me, had been unable to tell anyone what was happening outside the four walls of their house and, finding a total vacuum where information should be, have gone searching for answers online?

Chapter Fourteen

'Watch out for hate,
it can open its mouth and you'll fling yourself out
to eat off your leg, an instant leper.'

—Anne Sexton, 'Admonitions to a Special Person'

'You have to forgive your mother.'

I groaned and shook my head. 'Right . . .'

I was sitting in the green room at The Stand in Edinburgh with Raymond Mearns, a mercurial old redhead who'd been on the circuit for years. He normally shouted and swore a mile a minute on stage but had recently had therapy so now everyone backstage had to hear a working-class Glaswegian tell them how spiritually sick they were. It was my turn tonight after making a minor offhand comment about how much my mum annoyed me.

'Forgive your mother. It's for yer own good!'

When I got diagnosed, the doctor interviewed Mum and she came out with a list of my autistic traits going back to when I was a baby and punched the bars of my cot repeatedly when I woke up or cried when people touched me. I hadn't known about most of them.

In the summer of 2020, after the first lockdown was lifted, I was sent up to Scotland for some filming and planned to meet my mother in a Mexican restaurant in Glasgow city centre. Throughout lockdown, friends had said how excited they'd be to see their parents after a long period of enforced separation. I'd drawn an emotional blank when they said this but still made an attempt at mimicking their enthusiasm. The expectation of others had brought me here to meet my mother even though she did my head in and refused to use Google Maps. As usual, our meeting involved me trying not to shout at her as I verbally guided her round Glasgow and berated her for not answering her phone or knowing how to turn it off silent.

I remember going to a boyfriend's house years ago and watching his mum with his adult sister. The mother was sitting on the couch and his sister was on the floor while her mum stroked her hair. Something about the effortlessness of it, their unselfconscious mutual happiness, made me feel physically uncomfortable. Later I thought of the image over and over again, wondering if all women did that with their mothers. Sometimes Mum and I air-kissed if we met in cafes or restaurants (I'd avoided going to the house for years now) but anything beyond that made me feel frightened in a way I struggled to articulate.

Since my diagnosis we'd been looking at each other with fresh eyes.

'Mary from next door explained to me about autism in women – she had a job working with them – and it just *sounded* like you.' She looked down at her plate, frowning.

'Why was I not diagnosed at school, Mum? I was friends with a tree, I had meltdowns, I was doing all the classic autistic stuff.'

She began to concede, shaking her head *no, no, no*. 'I'm sorry! I always got you to do extracurricular stuff . . .Took you to bookshops and things as you just . . . You were always so *unhappy*, Fern! And I just wanted to try and help somehow.' She leaned forward in her chair, explaining.

I felt an unfamiliar jolt of sympathy; she sounded so panicked, as if it was all still happening. I thought back to the trouble with the police, of being kicked out, of stripping and all the change and the chaos. And the fact that all of this happened with parents who sent me to youth theatre, piano lessons, bookshops and art workshops. I thought of the hours and hours spent practising Mozart sonatas when I was depressed in my teens and how even now I still play piano as it's one of the only things that seems to latch onto both sides of my brain and distracts me from overwhelm and meltdowns. I'd kept on having the piano lessons even when Dad was making no money as a mechanic and we were skint.

I took a deep breath.

'I was reading about how many autistic people end up in the criminal-justice system or in and out of psych care their whole lives . . . And I keep thinking how different things would have been if you and Dad hadn't . . .'

I felt the discomfort of big emotion and stopped, looking down at the plate of tacos the waiter had just plonked on our table before I started talking again.

'Like, I still play piano today and if yous hadn't got me lessons I—'

I had to choke back the sobs. I wanted to say that I knew now she had been doing her best, which was insane as I'm not that type of person. I thought of teen me staring at her in the car on the way to Westleigh Way, promising to hate her forever. I couldn't break my promise to myself.

'If you hadn't . . .' I tried to start speaking again but the lump in my throat was now apple-sized. I felt frustrated that I couldn't communicate my emotions the way other women did. I looked around self-consciously. Glasgow is a village and I didn't want any of the audience from last night's show to spot me. Mum was openly weeping.

I pulled the COVID face mask over my face to hide the tears as we held each other's gaze. For the first time, I thought about having a baby that cried when you tried to cuddle her, a toddler that scowled when you talked to her and scratched her arms when you touched her.

I thought about this autistic kid I'd read about, Jacob Barnett. He was a physics genius but had been told as a kid he'd never have the ability to speak or tie his own shoelaces. His mum said she'd used a system called 'muchness', where she didn't force him to learn but encouraged him to pursue his intense interests. I realized Mum had intuitively done autism-friendly education. When I'd wanted to do Highers that were almost entirely foreign languages and Dad had mocked me and told me to do physics, she'd encouraged me. When I'd refused to do maths, she'd supported it. When I'd wanted to rent a beginner's guide to Danish from the library or paint Chinese characters on my bedroom wall or recite French verb drills for two hours at a time, she'd been there.

As we looked at each other now she told me about when she was working at her Tesco checkout and told a posh woman that her daughter was studying Arabic at Edinburgh University and the woman had done a double-take before regaining composure.

'Oh? You must be very proud.'

'You must be very patronizing,' Mum had shot back.

'I had a nice time with my mum,' I told Conor when I got back home to London.

Unexpectedly, I started to sob sat at the kitchen table.

'But I wish I didn't, because now when she dies I'll be sad – and before, I don't think I would have minded too much.' I made a face of surprise then said flatly: 'Sorry, I dunno why I'm crying.'

He patted me. 'Poor Fern: you've a lot of emotions and they make you feel confused.'

It's uncomfortable that this isn't all good or all bad or a happy ending or a sad ending, but just a mess that everyone muddled through. It's very painful to start loving someone when holding on to the idea of hating them keeps you safe.

This is the closest I can get to an uplifting conclusion.

I still have meltdowns and I still keep chipping away at

refining the data on what causes them and how I can try to solve them. I still exist in a work environment where I'm forced to mask because to expect accommodations would still be seen as asking too much in a world where most people still know next to nothing on my neurotype. I'll always have a sensory system that is wired differently; where a light touch makes me want to scratch my skin off, sudden noises cause me pain and fluorescent light feels like it's sucking the life out of me. The flipside is that music lights up every nerve in my body like a Christmas tree and I have a finely tuned ability to detect phoniness and hypocrisy where others fail to see it.

I'm also an autistic person now and not in another time where I'd have been institutionalized or trialled as a witch. I'm an autistic person in the UK and not in China, where they wouldn't even acknowledge either my autism or my subsequent mental illness.

I've accepted I may never have lasting friendships or know how to maintain them. I feel despair at the thought of having another relationship and introducing someone new to this mess. Soon it'll be menopause and the disruption to my hormones will send my oversensitive system madder than normal, just like any chemicals or drugs do. Then the increasing illness of middle age will mean navigating the minefield of dealing with doctors who misinterpret and misread autistic pain. After that I'll likely have to deal with being a neurodivergent person in an old folks' home that's been designed exclusively with neurotypical needs in mind and the exclusion and social problems will mean it'll be like school all over again.

But for now I have *you*. I've told you everything – I've spared you nothing because I know that if I'd kept anything back or secret I'd inadvertently be giving the message that it's shameful. I'm what some people call 'openly autistic' – a term I'm uncomfortable with because the 'open' part suggests it's odd that I'm not keeping quiet about it but maybe I should. All I can do is keep talking about it and hope you'll then go and make things feel better for the next autistic or misfit girl you meet. That doing all this will bring about tiny incremental changes is the only thing I have any certainty about.

Acknowledgements

Thanks to my publisher and editor Romilly Morgan for maintaining an unwavering sense of enthusiasm throughout the whole process and providing constant encouragement and cheerleading when I was sending her the bleakest parts of my life. I really had no idea the process would be so fun and that's entirely down to you.

Polly Poulter, Sybella Stephens and everyone at Octopus Publishing Group for working tirelessly to get the book over the line despite lots of roadblocks. Cheers to Kirsty Howarth for handling the legal stuff with grace and sensitivity.

Monica Hope was an unexpected delight: officially, she carried out the slickest of copy edits that made the final manuscript better than I could have hoped. Unofficially she was the source of fun phone chats in the middle of editing hell as well as providing lots of reassurance right up until the glue was drying on the proof copies.

Increasingly, I feel no one knows more about autism than other autistic people so thanks to Joanne Limburg, who as well as being a great inspiration to this newly diagnosed autistic, gave considered notes and gentle corrections when it came to some of my autism stats and research.

My comedy agents Chris Quaile and Brid Kirby at IAM offered vital early encouragement when I was too embarrassed to send the seedling chapters to anyone else. Thanks for also being tolerant of me cancelling multiple gigs over the course of a year in order to finish this thing.

Jess Molloy at Curtis Brown gave thoughtful, incisive editorial notes on the proposal that helped bring everything into focus and was a constant source of calm in the face of my worrying.

My pal Alison Spittle is endless kindness packed into a tiny Irish woman. Thanks for seeing my autistic traits and looking after me in social situations.

Thanks to Lauren for being there in the most important scenes as well as the wind beneath my wings.

To my parents, cheers for all the novels and library trips; I'm only sorry I wrote the exact kind of book you'd have confiscated from me when I was younger.

Dr Sue Smith is a genuine wonder woman and I feel lucky to have found the Lorna Wing Centre.

Biggest hugs to my partner Conor for both supporting me in pursuing a diagnosis, then listening to a daily, incessant stream of facts about autism for the next three years and only complaining once. You are the wisest and the kindest.

Most of all thanks to every young autistic influencer, TikToker and YouTuber who has disregarded the potential judgement and mockery of others to share vital information online in order to fill the complete void where health services and post-diagnostic support should be. You're all a force to be reckoned with and the source of much of my optimism.